THE S1NGLE PARENT FAMILY

THE S1NGLE PARENT FAMILY

For Helping Professionals and Parents

Edited By

Thomas D. Yawkey, Ph.D.
The Pennsylvania State University
University Park, PA 16802

Georgianna M. Cornelius, Ph.D.
New Mexico State University
Las Cruces, NM 88003

TECHNOMIC
PUBLISHING CO., INC.

LANCASTER · BASEL

The Single Parent Family

a **TECHNOMIC**®publication

Published in the Western Hemisphere by
Technomic Publishing Company, Inc.
851 New Holland Avenue
Box 3535
Lancaster, Pennsylvania 17604 U.S.A.

Distributed in the Rest of the World by
Technomic Publishing AG

Printed in the United States of America
10 9 8 7 6 5 4 3 2 1

Main entry under title:
   The Single Parent Family: For Helping Professionals and Parents

A Technomic Publishing Company book
Bibliography: p.
Index: p. 187

Library of Congress Card No. 89-51911
ISBN No. 87762-542-5

TO PROMOTING A better understanding of nontraditional families and the contributions they can make to positive and healthy development of their family members.

Table of Contents

Foreword

"THE SINGLE PARENT family" is a deceptive phrase. It seems so simple: a child or children living with one parent. In reality, the phrase may be used to indicate a divorced parent with a child, a widowed parent with children, an adoptive parent, a foster parent, or a biological parent living with children. The parent may be a father or a mother, teen-aged or middle-aged, single by choice or by chance. The "single parent family" may mean a parent living with children alone or it may mean a parent living with a child in the child's grandparents' house. What the phrase does not automatically indicate is a pathological environment for the child.

In the face of all the publicity and the sometimes horrified public outcry over the single parent family, it is vital to remember that single parent families are doing the same thing dual parent families are doing: they are trying to raise healthy, happy, well-adjusted children. Just as there can be deviant families with two parents, so there can be with one parent, but a single parent family is not, by definition, a diseased family form.

The prevalence of single parent families provokes questions about what constitutes a "normal" family. Phillipe Aries (1962) concluded that, until modern times, in western society, children were raised by the community. Perhaps the idea of a nuclear family consisting of a mother, a father, and children is a psychological defense mechanism. The nuclear family may be a myth which denies the existence of the extended family. This denial may have defended against the grief caused by the permanent separations of families due to the industrialization of 17th and 18th century Europe (Uzoka, 1979). We no longer need the myth to protect us because modern travel and communication can ensure that separations are temporary, but we have come to accept the myth as reality. This illusion now causes us grief as we realize that we need the support of a broadly based family system and as we see more non-nuclear family forms developing.

Because all of us, parents or not, need emotional support, we sometimes make our own extended families. Single parents may, of financial necessity, return to the homes of their own parents. Even if they don't make the physical move back to the homes of their childhood, single parents, in their search for social and emotional support, may choose to renew extended family ties. They may also build a new "family" through relationships with people who are not related by blood or by marriage.

Since most of us have grown up in a family, we may have a false confidence in our own knowledge of the family, and tend to generalize our own experiences to others. Now, as we are forced to the realization that single parent families are not transitory phenomena, it is time to look beyond our generalizations. What will research show us about the single parent family, about its weaknesses, and, more importantly, about its strengths?

David Elkind (1981) says that children from single parent families may too easily become "hurried" children because they must provide emotional support to the parent with whom they are living. In providing such support, which in a dual parent family would come from the second parent, the children may grow up too fast, missing the chance to act on the same developmental level as their peers. But in *any* family a child may be hurried too much and may be asked to become a confidante instead of a son or a daughter. Single parent families can develop emotional support systems so that their children can still be children. However, even with such a support system, the child is likely to have increased responsibilities in relation to the daily tasks of family living. If both the parent and the child perceive the responsibilities to be fair and positive, the result is likely to be increased self-esteem on the part of the child. The single parent family, out of necessity, may find it easier than the dual parent family to provide roles for its children as valuable, responsible family members.

Our society has stereotypes for the single parent—"unwed mother" or "teen-age parent"—but, as Cornelius and others show in this book, the stereotype is not the norm. It is time for our culture to make arrangements to suit single parent families as well as those with two parents. Perhaps this book will help us on our way.

References

ARIES, P. *Centuries of Childhood.* New York:Vantage Press (1962).

ELKIND, D. *The Hurried Child.* Menlo Park, CA:Addison-Wesley Publishing Company (1981).

UZOKA, A. F. "The Myth of the Nuclear Family: Historical Background and Clinical Implications," *American Psychologist*, 34(11):1095–1106 (1979).

HARRIET E. DARLING, PH.D.
Associate Professor of Education
Director, Juniata College Early
   Childhood Education Center
Huntingdon, PA

Preface

PROFESSIONAL ISSUES CONCERNING the changing family system are numerous. Realistically, a one-volume text can make no credible attempt to address thoroughly all issues of import. However, the present volume does succeed in presenting data that clearly delineate the social, economic, and personal changes in the American family.

The needs of parent and child are explored directly through numerous research studies from a variety of disciplines and the results presented clearly in the chapters. The contributing authors of the present text are engaged in both investigative and applied vocations. All contributing authors have conducted pertinent and practical research in working with parents and children.

GEORGIANNA M. CORNELIUS, PH.D.
New Mexico State University

Acknowledgements

"LABOR OF LOVE" is frequently an epithet applied to academic works, and the present volume is no exception. The editors are deeply indebted to the authors and co-authors of the chapters of this book for their professionalism and interest in the topic. Their contributions, names, affiliations, and addresses are listed in the *Contributors* section. All completed their work without financial compensation, but with the awareness that their additions to the literature on new modes of parenting would provide a sound research basis for those whose vocation it is to counsel single parents and their children.

In addition, the editors also appreciate the interest in the topic of single parent families exhibited by personnel of the book's publisher. These include Mr. Melvyn Kohudic, President; Mr. Richard Dunn, Vice President of Marketing; Mr. Joseph Eckenrode, Editor; Ms. Barbara Jones, Administrative Secretary; and Mr. Anthony Deraco, Manager/Production and Graphics–Technomic Publishing Company, Inc., Lancaster, PA.

PART I

Trends in the Family Structure

THE FOCUS OF the following section is on the changing structure of the family. Naively, we think of family in terms of a core nucleus consisting of father, mother, and children. For many others, the family is thought of in terms of an extended family with grandparents, aunts, and uncles. Such a given picture dissolves as we look more closely at our radically changing culture. Conceptually, the changes are complex and varied. The contributing authors identify and discuss this changing family structure and how these changes relate to children. In addition, the contributing authors investigate how these changes affect the family. Jaun Ramon Morales-Flores explores the father-headed household, while Georgianna M. Cornelius examines the mother-headed family system.

The following two chapters examine the single parent family system with the father and mother as the head of household and conceptualize seven critical areas. The conceptual issues of interest discussed are: (a) impact of divorce, (b) changing social attitudes, (c) the role and responsibilities of the single parent, (d) differences in mother- versus father-headed households, (e) economic changes, (f) social issues; and (g) development and behavior of young children in single parent households.

Morales-Flores focuses on the alternative family forms involving the father as the primary caregiver in the home, while Cornelius examines the single female parent household. Both authors discuss and review the number of alternative family forms, and the variety of reasons underlying these new family forms. Interestingly, both authors examine the census data that single out the increasing rate of divorce with children and the changing attitudes of young

1

couples. Each of these concepts is discussed in the following sections.

More couples are waiting longer to have children, while others choose not to marry and yet to have children. Also, values have dramatically changed such that a large number of young adults are choosing careers over marriage and then later adopting children. The alternative forms are clearly delineated in the two chapters, and the implications of this changing family structure are discussed.

Impact of Divorce

The authors target divorce as the primary reason for many single parent households, while teenage pregnancy is an important social dilemma. The number of teenagers making the important choice of keeping their babies has created thousands of single parent households.

The number of parents in the home changes and transforms the ''accepted'' norm of what constitutes a family. Both authors parallel the viewpoint that such changes in family structure do not constitute a fragmented family, but a new, very pronounced family structure which involves a large portion of our population. Cornelius extends this issue by describing this new structure through a set of complex issues ranging from economics to custody rights.

Attitudes

As a result of the large number of single parent families, attitudes in parenting have radically changed. For example, issues of custody, visitation, and support have taken on extreme importance for families and for professionals in education. How do we as teachers effectively recognize and meet the needs of young children from single parent households? As education professionals, we need to inquire: do these children have special needs? And if so, what are they? Are the attitudes toward more single parenting positive or negative ones? As a society, do we treat these new ''parents'' as less than a family? And more importantly, are the children from these new alternative family forms treated differently?

Attitudes regarding who rears the children are changing tremendously. Morales-Flores clearly points out that many fathers have very positive interactions with young children. Morales-Flores supports this with research studies documenting father competency skills while Cornelius argues that census data still documents the majority of young children of divorce as reared in mother-headed households. Jointly, the two chapters crystallize the reality that more and more complex decisions are to be made regarding young children. The number of choices for a new lifestyle are varied and complex. These choices are frequently chosen alone, and the decisions are frequently implemented alone.

Issues of the child's acceptance in society are not reviewed, but the difficulty for family adjustment is discussed. The changing attitudes of adults in their decisions to marry, not to marry, or even divorce are clearly documented and the trend towards different family structures is made clear.

Roles and Responsibilities

The alternative family structures involve dramatic changes in the role and responsibility of the single parent. With this new role, many adults are facing multiple demanding responsibilities of parenting alone. There are sharp differences between the single mother-headed household and father-headed households. These differences are discussed by the contributing authors as educational, economic, and social. The authors point out that the new single parent now faces multiple roles and responsibilities which alter past lifestyles, standards of living, and attitudes. For example, both men and women as single parents face ''super parent'' expectations from society, stress and guilt if they fail in the process, and continual life strain. On the other hand, the multiple roles have created a very strong trend towards increased attention on parenting and the responsibilities involved as a result of divorce. More adults are realizing that parenting is a learned process of growth and skill in development.

The authors hint at the need for ''parent'' growth in rearing children, but the two chapters clearly identify the need for education in parenting.

Cornelius reports that, educationally and economically, fathers have been shown to be better prepared than single mothers in heading a household. The responsibility of assuming these new tasks seems to represent a greater adjustment for the woman based on the lack of preparation in life. The multiple tasks of parenting delineated by both authors reflect the same needs found in dual parent households. Such responsibilities in raising children are numerous and complex.

Differences in Mother- versus Father-Headed Households

The differences in mother- and father-headed households is examined with respect to economic conditions, parenting roles, and interaction with young children. Morales-Flores cites supporting evidence focusing on the competence of the father in parenting and points out numerous studies on the importance of the father in child development. Similarly, Cornelius addresses the issues of stress, low economic conditions, and lack of stability in mother-headed households.

Differences are sharpened by economic gaps in income, changes in housing, and standard of living. Differences are also defined in terms of communication, rough and tumble play, and dependency issues of young children.

Economic Changes

The majority of single parent households function primarily on one income source. Frequently, if support is involved, it goes unpaid, and the new family income decreases to a lower economic category. Even when the support is paid to many families, these payments do not equal the original household's double income.

In the following chapters, economic changes are discussed in terms of housing, foods, products, and services. For example, leisure activities are cited as a family change. For example, the single parent family may not be able to afford swimming or piano lessons.

Social Issues

The social status of the single parent has been identified as a very critical societal issue involving self-esteem and acceptance. The authors clarify the difficult demands of parenting and the limited time for "parent" activities and personal growth.

For many married adults who have for one reason or another become single parents, the adjustment period to being alone is a difficult one. This adjustment period is frequently perceived as one of difficulty, and many parents report depressions and isolation. With regard to divorce or separation, research has shown the period shortly following the divorce as one of guilt and anger.

The complex issues that precede a divorce or the reasons why an adult selects single parenting can easily be translated into multiple texts of information. The following chapters focus on the feelings of isolation and the social well-being of the parent. What both authors point out is that parenting engages a great deal of the parent, psychologically and physically. The single parent is now faced with the critical need of preserving his or her own mental health.

The authors discuss socialization, inasmuch as important problems of seeking out new friendships, maintaining old ones, and restructuring one's life are shared by both men and women. However, there are differences in that women seek more intimate, long lasting friendships more often than men do. Also, for many single women who have not had an active working or social life, going out is sometimes a difficult task, whereas, for many men who have been in the work force, the risk of meeting new people is less threatening. In addition, the need for support systems is quite clearly pointed out in the two chapters. Morales notes the specific needs of the father in relation to other adults, while Cornelius similarly supports this notion of social networks and helping others in mother-headed families.

The Development and Behaviors of Young Children

The authors pointedly discuss the changes in young children's behavior following a divorce and of being a child in a single parent household. During the crisis children are reported as severely affected by what the parents do and how parents handle the situation. Because of the emotional intensity, children experience trauma and their behavior is discussed in that vein.

Issues of development for both boys and girls is reviewed through numerous research studies (e.g., Hetherington, Cox, and Cox, 1979; Lamb, 1982). Morales-Flores and Cornelius discuss the methodological issues of how economics, duration of crisis, and communication of parent and child need further examination.

Summary

Families headed by single parents are obviously growing in number. What seems clear are the emerging differences in households headed by single men and women.

The beliefs and attitudes regarding single parents need further research and social attentions. The authors have examined: (a) the impact of divorce, (b) changing social attitudes, (c) the role and responsibilities of the single parent, (d) differences in mother- versus father-headed households, (e) economic changes, (f) social issues of the single parent, and (g) development and behavior of young children in single parent households.

As our culture grows through multiple changes, the family of our future will reflect these changes. The complexity of single parenting and the development of young children will require further examination.

References

HETHERINGTON, E., M. Cox and R. Cox. "Effects of Divorce on Parents and Children," in *Nontraditional Families: Parenting and Child Development*, M. E. Lamb, ed., Lawrence Erlbaum Associates, Inc. (1982).

LAMB, M. E. *Nontraditional Families: Parenting and Child Development*. Lawrence Erlbaum Associates, Inc. (1982).

CHAPTER 1

Role of the Male Parent as Father in Nontraditional Families

JUAN R. MORALES-FLORES

Introduction

CHANGES IN SOCIOECONOMIC aspects of the world have created modifications in all levels of society. Sex roles have somewhat
changed and with them the duties and activities associated with
each sex in the family setting. This includes the father taking a
more active role in parenting and in the caretaking of young
children (Chibucos and Kail, 1981; Hanson, 1981). These facts have
motivated research studies of the father–child interaction and the
father as a source of nurturance and love (i.e., Greif, 1985; Hanson,
1981; Levy-Shiff, Sharir, and Mogilner, 1989; Radin and Harold-
Goldsmith, 1989; Tauber, 1979). Some of these research studies
revealed that the father can take care of children, including infants,
as competently as the mother does (Sawin and Parke, 1979). The
father not only seems to be as competent as the mother (Belsky,
1979; Chibucos and Kail, 1981), his interaction and play with the
child seem to be more active, thus stimulating both the social and
cognitive development of the youngster (Chibucos and Kail, 1981;
Lamb 1976a). Opposite to what might be predicted, when fathers are
nurturant and participate in children caretaking, the masculinity of
sons and the femininity of daughters are greater (Lamb, 1976a).

In addition, the structure of the family has changed. At present,
there are more single parent families than ever before (U.S. Census,
1988). Meanwhile, the number of fathers who are obtaining custody
of their children is increasing (Collins, 1979; Hanson, 1981). Motivated by these changes, different studies have been conducted in
order to get more information regarding the influence of the father
in a child's development. However, new variables have been con-

sidered in these studies. For example, single parent families have been compared with standard, dual parent families. Likewise, single mother families, single father families, and other variations of single father families, such as single father and stepmother families, have been similarly compared. This chapter deals primarily with research performed in single father families and in intact families where the father is the primary caregiver.

Research on the Father in Child Rearing

Father-Custody Families

In recent years, more fathers in divorce situations have been awarded custody of their children (Collins, 1979; Hanson, 1981). The father usually obtained custody when the mother was proved to be unfit (Santrock, Warshak, and Elliot, 1982). However, the custody decision processes are changing and the benefits to the children and other factors are considered now before awarding the custody to one of the parents.

Santrock, et al. (1982) studied the social development of children in father-custody families by contrasting them with children in mother-custody and intact families. Sixty-four white, predominantly middle class families with children between six and eleven years were studied. Half of the children were boys and half were girls. The sample was divided into three groups: one-third of the children came from families in which the custody was awarded to the father, one-third came from families in which the custody was awarded to the mother, and one-third came from intact families. Results of analyses of variance on the matching variables revealed no significant group differences (Santrock et al., 1982).

Santrock et al. (1982) used a multimethod approach to obtain data for studying family interaction: (1) observing parents (in the intact family group, the mother and the father took part on different days) and children interaction during a laboratory session; (2) observing each child while being interviewed; (3) administering structured interviews and self-report scales to parents and children; (4) giving a projective task to both parents and children; and (5) asking teachers about their perceptions of the children.

The parent and the child were asked to plan an activity together and to discuss the main problems of the family. These were videotaped for ten minutes each. The parent–child interactions were classified on nine-point scales (two scales were used, one for parents and one for children). These ranged from one (child controls the parent, parent has no control over child) to nine (consistent control of the parent over the child). Based on observations of parent–child interaction in the laboratory, Santrock et al. (1982) found that "boys showed more problems in social development than girls in mother-custody families" (p. 293). However, in father-custody families, boys showed more competent social behavior than girls (Santrock et al., 1982, p. 293). Santrock et al. (1982) stated that:

> Significant differences were found on four of the child dimensions— boys whose fathers have custody were less demanding than girls in this type of family structure, whereas, girls were less demanding than boys in mother-custody families. A similar, significantly positive same-sex-child-and-parent effect was shown in the children's maturity, sociality, and independence [p. 293].

A 4 × 2 analysis of variance test was conducted in order to evaluate the observations of parent–child interactions.

> The factors were: family structure (mother with custody, father with custody; mother in intact family; father in intact family); and sex of child. Duncan Multiple Range Tests were used to specify the effects revealed by the ANOVAS [Santrock et al., 1982, p. 296].

Santrock et al. (1982) stated that "significant main effects occurred for controlling [$F(3,66) = 5.22, p < .003$] and permissive [$F(3,66) = 5.71, p < .002$] parenting orientations" (p. 296). Some of the conclusions of Santrock et al. (1982) were that "mothers with custody were more likely to allow the child to control them ($\overline{X} = 4.05$) than were fathers with custody ($\overline{X} = 6.00$), and intact-family mothers ($\overline{X} = 6.06$) and fathers ($\overline{X} = 6.12$)" (p. 296). They also concluded that adequate social behavior is more characteristic of the child whose custodial parent is the same sex.

The study discussed in this section presents how the father figure in father-custody families will have different effects on his children, depending on their sex. It seems that children from divorced families would be better off if custody is given to the parent of the same sex. Also it seems clear at this point that fathers with an active role in child caring and rearing are providing a richer, more complete environment for their children's social and cognitive development.

In a research conducted by Hetherington, Cox, and Cox (1982) dealing with the effects of divorce on parents and children, the results show changes in the families' members' behaviors at different periods of time (i.e., two months, one year, two years). Separate repeated measures of multivariate analyses of variance were performed involving test sessions, sex of child, family group (i.e., divorced versus non-divorced), and level of conflict for the set of measures from each data source. It was found that "the pattern of differences between groups changes markedly over the course of the two-year period following divorce" (Hetherington et al., 1982, p. 261). During the period of time before two years, things seemed to become worse for the divorced parents and children before they started to get better. The divorced father initially began by being extremely permissive with the children and becoming very restrictive over the two-year period (Hetherington et al., 1982). This behavior of the father seemed to enhance development of aggressive behaviors in boys but not in girls. However, no significant evidence was found that linked these behaviors specifically to the father figure. It seemed to be more an effect of the whole divorce situation.

Father as Primary Caregiver

There are a number of current studies on the effects of single father families. They are reviewed in the following section. A study was conducted in order to explore some possible antecedents and consequences of paternal child rearing in middle class, intact, primarily white families. Radin (1982) selected the sample for this study as follows: (1) fifty-nine intact, middle class families and (2) fifty-eight white and one Asian, with children three to six years of age. There were thirty-two boys and twenty-seven girls in the study. All fathers were actively involved in child care. Father's average age was thirty-four years. Radin (1982) divided the sample according to the amount of father involvement in child rearing following the responses of parents to questions in five different areas. These areas were: (1) statements of father's involvement in child care, (2) father's responsibility for physical child care, (3) father's responsibility for socialization of the child, (4) father's involvement in decision making regarding the child, and (5) father's availability to the child (Radin, 1982). The total of these five components was labeled the Paternal Involvement in Child Care Index (Radin, 1982). The father's total involvement score and the mother's total involvement score were added together producing a total involvement score. The families were divided into three subgroups: (a) The Father Primary Caregiver Group (those with the highest scores); (b) The Mother Primary Caregiver Group (those with the lowest scores), containing twenty families each; and (c) an Intermediate Group (those with the middle scores), containing nineteen families.

The procedure in Radin's study (1982) consisted of three appointments with each of the families. In the first appointment the father was interviewed at home and for approximately one hour with the child present only. The interview was audiotape-recorded. The second interview took place with the mothers either at home or at work, with nobody else present. The same questions asked of the fathers were asked of the mothers. A series of tasks were administered to the child during a third interview at home. Eight different measures were administered to the children: (1) Stanford Preschool Interval-External Scale (SPIES), (2) the Stephens-Delys Test of Internality, (3) the revised It-Scale, (4) the Parent Role Perception Test (PRPT), (5) a shortened version of the Kagan Parent Role Test, (6) Borke's Empathy Test, (7) the Peabody Picture Vocabulary Test, and (8) the Ravens Coloured Progressive Matrices Test (Radin, 1982).

The results of the study indicated that "mothers' views of fathers' involvement in child care correlated significantly with fathers' statements of their involvement ($r = .51$, $p < .001$), and mothers' statements of fathers' involvement were significantly associated with the fathers' perceptions of their role in child care ($r = .56$, $p < .001$)" (Radin, 1982, p. 183). The father's role in decision making was the only component of this study in which mothers' and fathers' perceptions of the fathers' role in child care tend to disagree (Radin, 1982). A positive relationship was observed between paternal involvement and the verbal ability of children. A significant association between paternal child-rearing measures and potential consequences in the subsample of girls was found. The father–daughter association may be either positive or negative. As the involvement by fathers in child care became greater and it was more likely that fathers were perceived as more punitive and more salient, this was also positively associated with verbal ability in girls. Radin (1982) stated:

> The findings suggest that men heavily involved in raising their preschoolers will spend more time in efforts to stimulate the children's cognitive growth, particularly with their daughters. However, their direct teaching activities still appear to be focused on sons, not daughters [p. 201].

The father's involvement in child care appears to be associated with greater internality for both sons and daughters.

Sagi (1982) conducted a study with three major populations: urban Jewish families, rural Druze (independent religious and ethnic group in Israel) families, and Kibbutz (cooperative community) families. He considered: (1) the components of paternal involvement as: (a) physical child care, (b) responsibility for socialization process, (c) decision making, and (d) father's availability; (2) the factors affecting the degree of parental involvement (i.e., father's recollections of their own father's involvement); and (3) the effects on children of varying degrees of paternal involvement. The data was obtained from both parents and children.

For the data from urban families, a large middle class suburb of Haifa was selected. Intact families that were selected had two children. Families needed to have at least one child that was between three and six years old. These were the subjects. Using a short questionnaire completed by parents, Sagi (1982) established the amount of time that each parent was involved with the child. Only families in which both parents agreed on the amount of time that the father was involved in child care were selected. Sixty families were included in the final data: (1) fifteen families had the father more involved; (2) in twenty families, both were equally involved; and (3) in twenty-five families, the mother was more involved.

The fathers were asked to indicate: (1) the extent of their involvement in child care and (2) their own father's involvement in child rearing when they were children. They were asked to indicate their satisfaction with their father's involvement in two ways: (1) their adult perspective and (2) their recollections of what they felt as children. The Israeli project, as the research is known, examined four areas of child development. These areas were empathy, independence, achievement, and locus of control. The Israeli project defined empathy as a type of social competence. Children of high-involved fathers scored highest on the Empathy Test used by the Project, followed by the children in the intermediate group, and children of low-involved fathers in that same order. The differences were significant. Sagi (1982) concluded that fathers contribute more to the children's development of empathy as their involvement in child rearing increases.

Regarding the locus of control, it was assessed by direct testing of the child. The Stanford Preschool Internal-External Scale was completed by the children, and the Torgoff Developmental Timetable was administered to the fathers (in order to get information regarding independence and achievement). Sagi (1982) found the following:

Children of fathers with intermediate and high involvement exhibited significantly ($F2.54 = 12.01$, $p < .001$) more internal locus of control ($M = 7.35$ and $M = 8.25$, respectively) than children of fathers with low involvement ($M = 5.70$). This applied to both boys and girls. Moreover, fathers with intermediate and high involvement reported that they encouraged achievement (M intermediate $= 60.75$ and M high $= 57.47$) and independence (M intermediate $= 60.52$ and M high $= 57.60$) in their sons and daughters earlier ($F2.54 = 34.48$, $p < .001$ for achievement; $F2.54 = 30.43$, $p < .001$ for independence) than did fathers with low involvement (M achievement $= 83.57$ and M independence $= 81.92$). The findings consistently showed that highly involved fathers had high expectations of their children on instrumental measures and that they encouraged development in this direction [p. 220–221].

The It-Scale was used to measure the children's gender orientation, and the Kagan Parent Role Test was utilized to examine the children's perceptions of their fathers. The results showed that paternal involvement influenced the scores of the children on the It-scale test (Sagi, 1982). "Children in the groups with intermediate and high paternal involvement scored higher in masculinity ($F2.54 = 9.74$, $p < .001$) than children in the groups of low paternal involvement ($Ms = 51.00$; 47.30; 38.3 respectively)" (Sagi, 1982, p. 222). Only for girls, an effect of paternal involvement was found. Daughters of fathers with intermediate and high involvement scored higher on the masculinity aspect than did daughters of low-involved fathers, although their scores still remained on the feminine range.

The data obtained in the Druze and the Kibbutz study regarding the fathers' opinions about their male parents indicate that fathers surpass their fathers' involvement primarily in areas of nurturance and physical care in the Druze. In the two systems of the Kibbutz (i.e., familiar systems and collective system), the fathers scored significantly higher than their fathers.

Father and Mother Interaction Patterns

A study dealing with interactions between seven- and eight-month-old infants and their fathers and mothers was performed by Lamb (1976). The purpose of this study was to observe: (1) the children forming their first social attachments and (2) the development of patterns of interaction with the two parents. Lamb (1976) focused on two classes of interaction: (1) play and (2) physical contact. The subjects were ten boys, ten girls, and their parents.

The infants were observed twice (once at seven months old and at eight months old) at home in the presence of both parents. A Visitor (V) who interacted with the family in a casual way and an Observer (O) who dictated into a tape recorder in detail the infant's behavior and the behavior of the other people, were to be present. The V's purpose was to make parents feel more relaxed and to offer the infant another alternative of an adult with whom to interact. The V did not focus attention on the child. Each visit lasted between one and two hours.

The scores of each infant were converted to rates per minute in order to perform analyses. Lamb (1976) used a repeated-measures' multivariate analysis of variance (MANOVA) which used the rates of smiling, vocalizing, looking, laughing, touching, fussing, reaching, seeking to be held, approaching, and proximity as variables. These analyses assessed whether there was a consistent preference for any of the subjects (mother, father, or visitor) at the time of the visit.

Regarding the interactions (i.e., play and physical contact), there was no greater number of play episodes either with fathers or mothers. However, the response to play with fathers was significantly more positive than to play with mothers ($X_F^2 = 4.9$, $X_M^2 = 4.4$, $p < .05$) (Lamb, 1976). Lamb (1976) found that "although fathers did not play for a significantly greater amount of time nor engaged in more frequent play sequences than the visitor, the average duration of each ($X_F^2 = 3.0$, $X_V^2 = 2.3$, $p < .05$) and the average response ($X_V^2 = 4.1$, $p < .01$) were greater in the father–infant interactions" (p. 319). Also, the fathers used physical games and idiosyncratic games more frequently than the mother. A tendency to initiate more play with girls than with boys was shown by mothers, while fathers did not show any preference.

In the area of physical contact, the mother tended to pick up the infant more frequently than the fathers and for longer periods of time. However, the child responded more positively to physical contact with the father. Lamb (1976) found that:

> The reason . . . may lie in the fact that caretaking ($p < .01$ for number, $p < .05$ for duration) and discipline/control ($p < .05$ for number, $p < .05$ for duration) holds were much more common with the mothers, whereas a much greater portion of the time during which the infants were held by their fathers was for the purpose of play ($p < .001$) [p. 221].

Natural Father–Stepmother Families

Santrock, Warshak, and Elliot (1982) conducted a study in social development and parent–child interaction in stepmother families and compared these with father-custody families and intact families. They expected that boys would show less competent social behavior in stepmother families than in father-custody families. Data from forty out of sixty-four children and their families (from the first part of this study described on the Father-Custody Families section in this chapter) were utilized (twenty father-custody families and twenty matched intact families). Twenty children (ten boys and ten girls) who were living with their natural father and stepmother were also studied in a second part of their research. "A 3 × 2 analysis of variance was performed on the observations of the child's behavior during interaction with his or her father, with family structure (father-custody, stepmother, and intact) and sex of child as main factors" (Santrock et al., 1982, p. 307). Santrock et al. (1982) found that:

> Less affectionate behavior was shown with the father in stepmother than in father-custody and intact families ($p < .01$). However, a significant interaction effect for warmth suggested that less affection was displayed by boys with their father in stepmother families than boys in father-custody and girls in intact families ($p < .01$) [p. 308].

It was found also that:

> A number of sex-of-child effects indicated that boys showed less competent social behavior than girls. And two significant interaction effects revealed that intact-family boys were lower in self-esteem than the other three groupings of children ($p < .01$) and that intact-family girls were less demanding than the other three groups ($p < .05$) [Santrock et al., 1982, p. 309].

Conclusion

There appear to be several elements that the father male figure brings to development of social, cognitive, and motor development of children (Chibucos, et al., 1981; Lamb, 1976; Radin, 1986; Santrock et al., 1982). Sagi (1981, p. 204) stated this, ". . . increased paternal involvement directly affects the development of empathy, internal locus of control, sex-role orientation, and perception of fathers on the part of young children." Fathers are more likely than mothers to engage in dynamic play, stimulating an earlier development of cognitive and social skills in the children. Fathers tend to treat boys differently from girls, encouraging physical activity only for boys (Tauber, 1979). Fathers' play seems to be more unusual and more enjoyable, holding the infants' attention longer than mothers' play does (Lamb, 1976). They also present more stimulating materials to their daughters. The father as caregiver at home seems to increase the number of educational materials for his daughter, more than the mother, despite her being more available for the mastering of new skills by her daughter (Radin, 1982). Because of these differences, the role of the father seems to be more critical than the role of the mother in the selection of children's play and the perpetuation of sex differences.

It appears that high paternal involvement is associated with verbal ability of children and greater internality of both sons and daughters (Radin, 1982). It is believed that the simple interaction of the fathers with their children added a tension element (i.e., tension introduction) to the child. This may be due to the similarities in child-rearing duties, but differences in performance of these by the father in relation to the mother. It would be necessary to perform longitudinal studies in order to do observation and to document the consistency of fathers' child-rearing behaviors and possible long-term effects of these behaviors on their children.

References

BELSKY, J. "Mother-Father-Infant Interaction: A Naturalistic Observational Study," *Developmental Psychology*, 15(6):691–697 (1979).

CHIBUCOS, T. R. and P. R. Kail. "Longitudinal Examination of Father-Infant Interaction and Infant-Father Attachment," *Merrill-Palmer Quarterly*, 27(2):81–96 (1981).

COLLINS, G. "A New Look at Life with Father," *The New York Times*, 30–31; 49–50; 52, 65–66 (1979).

GREIF, G. L. "Practice with Single Fathers," *Social Work in Eduation*, 7(4):231–243 (1985).

HANSON, S. M. H. "Single Custodial Fathers (Report No. CG 016 271)," Milwaukee, WI:Washington State University, Intercollegiate Center for Nursing Education (ERIC Document Reproduction Service No. ED 222 805) (1981).

LAMB, M. E. "Interactions Between Eight-Month-Old Children and Their Fathers and Mothers," in *The Role of the Father in Child Development*, M. E. Lamb, ed., New York:Wiley (1976).

LAMB, M.E. "The Role of the Father: An Overview," in *The Role of the Father in Child Development*, M. E. Lamb, ed., New York:Wiley (1976a).

LEVY-SHIFF, R., H. Sharir, and M. B. Mogilner. "Mother- and Father-Preterm Infant Relationship in the Hospital Preterm Nursery," *Child Development*, 60:93–102 (1989).

RADIN, N. "Primary Caregiving and Role-Sharing Fathers," in *Nontraditional Families: Parenting and Child Development*, M. E. Lamb, ed., Hillsdale, NJ:Lawrence Erlbaum Associates, Publishers (1982).

RADIN, N. and R. Harold-Goldsmith. "The Involvement of Selected Unemployed and Employed Men with Their Children," *Child Development*, 60:454–459 (1989).

SAGI, A. "Antecedents and Consequences of Various Degrees of Paternal Involvement in Child Rearing: The Israeli Project," in *Nontraditional Families: Parenting and Child Development*, M. E. Lamb, ed., Hillsdale, NJ:Lawrence Erlbaum Associates (1986).

SANTROCK, B. T., R. A. Warshak, and G. L. Elliott. "Social Development and Parent-Child Interaction in Father-Custody and Stepmother Families," in *Nontraditional Families: Parenting and Child Development*, M. E. Lamb, ed., Hillsdale, NJ: Lawrence Erlbaum Associates (1982).

SAWIN, D. B. and R. D. Parke. "Father's Affectionate Stimulation and Caregiving Behaviors with Newborn Infants," *The Family Coordinator*, 33:509–513 (1979).

TAUBER, M. A. "Sex Differences in Parent–Child Interaction Styles During a Free-Play Session," *Child Development*, 50:981–988 (1979).

U.S. Census. *Population Characteristics*. U.S. Department of Commerce, Bureau of Census (1988).

CHAPTER 2

Mother-Headed Households

GEORGIANNA M. CORNELIUS

Introduction

THE SINGLE PARENT is a mom. The statement seems simple, clear, and to the point, but the concept is much more involved and complex. It conveys a family structure that is rapidly increasing and a situation of only one adult parenting one or more children.

The parent may be single for a variety of reasons. Single parenting may be the result of a death of a spouse or the result of separation or divorce. Single parent situations are common among many military families where the father is absent for long periods of time. The single mother may be single by choice if she elected not to marry yet chose to have children. Recently, many young women are choosing to adopt young children after their career has stabilized. The reality is a society of many single parents. The parent is single, solo, alone, and most frequently a female. She is primarily responsible for a multitude of tasks. In addition, this involves living alone as an adult, a parent, and sharing this with one or more children.

Statistics reveal that of the four and a half million families with a single female head, the woman has always been single in 12 percent, separated in 27 percent, divorced in 38 percent, widowed in 18 percent, and alone for other reasons in 5 percent (Brooks, 1985). According to recent 1985 statistics data, the trend for today's young adult is to postpone marriage to a median age of 25.5 years for men and 23.3 for women. Although this does not seem surprising, it is the highest median age for women ever recorded in history. What is surprising and quite shocking is the total number of women who do marry, have children, and later divorce. According to the 1985 census

17

data, 10.1 million female family households exist where there is no husband present and only 2.2 million male family households with no wife present.

In fact, according to the earlier census data of 1984, single parent households for all races totaled 8,544 as compared to only 3,808 in 1970. Those families maintained by the mother in 1984 numbered 7,599. In 1970, the number of mother-headed households equaled 3,415. In less than fifteen years, the number of female-headed households doubled. Single parent families headed by the father equaled 945 in 1984 and only 393 in 1970. (All numbers are in thousands.)

What we are seeing is a dramatic and consistent increase in the number of single parent families and the number of households headed by women. Unfortunately, along with this increase, we are witnessing an increased number of children who will spend a large portion of their young life without the father in the home.

The reasons for the dissolution of a household are many. However, divorce appears to be the greatest documented reason for this change.

Divorce

Divorce was identified as the primary cause of family dissolution, and its increase is well researched. The census data for 1984 show that for divorced persons per 1000 married persons, there has been a steady increase among persons of white, black, and Spanish origin. Statistics show, for the white race, 113 divorces per thousand, for the black race, 240, and for those of Spanish origin, 112. Divorce was found to be the most frequent between the ages of thirty-five and forty-five for all races.

Certainly, one can speculate the variety of reasons for divorce. Legally, it is relatively more easy to apply, file, and complete the proceedings of a divorce than it was ten years ago. Also, the choices for adults in lifestyle and personal choices are greater than ever before. Another reason may be the ever increasing stress caused by emotional and financial issues in the family. The rapidly changing pressures of the economy make financial stability a very stressful issue for many young couples, particularly those with young children.

Alternative social trends and lifestyles are appearing which diversify the issues of marriage and child rearing. Many more couples are living together and raising a number of children without the legal commitment of marriage. Still others are marrying much later in life. Finally, an increasing number of teenagers under the age of eighteen are becoming pregnant and keeping their children.

Number of Children under Eighteen

The number of children affected by this incredible increase of divorce is devastating. The number of children under the age of eighteen affected by the termination of a marriage is shocking. For every one child under eighteen living with one parent in a male-headed household, there are forty-four children of this age living in single parent, female-headed families. There are multiple reasons for the extreme difference in numbers. Culturally, our society emphasizes the need for the children to be living with the mother during the early developmental years. However, research has increasingly shown the need for both parents and adults to be actively involved in child rearing.

The department of public assistance through federal and state government programs aids the single parent in caring for dependent children in a variety of ways. Alimony and child support help defray the cost of raising children alone. However, alimony and child support do not fill the devastating gap of financial needs of the single female parent. Generally, court ordered child support petitions pass with a very minimum amount for the single parent. Frequently, absent fathers are difficult to locate and their payments sporadically paid, if at *all*. The process of petitioning for increases in support and for the spouse to pay consistently is cumbersome and ineffective. Many frustrated single parents who are struggling to maintain the household never see any support payments at *all!*

The number of single parents as heads of households has drastically increased in the last five years. There are three major differences in single and dual parent family structures that relate to the social and cognitive development of children. They are: (a) economic differences, (b) accessibility of adult support, and (c) increased parental role strain.

Economic Issues

There are economic issues that are specifically an issue for the single mother. Following a separation or divorce, the mother is faced with the crisis issue of supporting a family alone. This entails major adjustments involving bitterness and drastic changes in quality of living standards. The financial resources of the mother are meager and limited for several reasons. First, she has usually been a full- or part-time mother with little or no work experience. Frequently, she is at a disadvantage educationally because she has not invested her time and energy in securing higher education. Training in a specialized skill area is rare for the single mother for often she did not anticipate pursuing a career. Unfortunately, a large part of these problems stem from our society's practice of not consistently encouraging women to be assertive and independent in the work world. Women are not encouraged to set goals, priorities, or plan a career. For those encouraged to pursue a career, the choices are dictated and frequently limited.

Financially, within the marriage, the husband usually budgets the income, handles the economic responsibilities, and takes the leadership role in decision making. Financially, women may be ill-prepared to assume such responsibilities and lack the training and education to improve their situation. Census data over the last ten years consistently demonstrate that greater numbers of female-headed households are living in poverty and remaining at a poverty level income.

Weiss (1984) examined household income, income sources, and food and housing expenditures in families following marital dissolution. Specifically, the study focused on how household income is reduced after marital dissolution and the ways in which the post-dissolution household adapts economically. Approximately 5,000 cases were selected from the Michigan Panel Study of Income Dynamics (Mott, 1979). From the sample, 3,000 families were selected and considered representative of the United States population, and the remaining 2,000 were low-income households.

Interviews were conducted yearly over a twelve-year period with the heads of household. A married comparison sample was formed by taking all married mothers whose marriages had persisted for an interval of seven years. Analysis of this data showed that separation and divorce brought about reduction of income in every income category. The reduction was greatest when the marital income was high. In fact, the income levels of the separated and divorced stayed constant thoughout the five-year interval after the marital dissolution. Marital dissolution decreases the average income following divorce, and the income level remains low. The economic consequences resulting from divorce have direct implications for the family members. First, in all income categories the reduction in income appeared to persist indefinitely as long as the household remained headed by female single parents (Weiss, 1984).

The census data from 1985 show consistent findings locating female single parents primarily in middle- to low-income categories. Also, a prolonged reduction in income for a growing family with increasing costs has a high cost for the children and the mother. Limited incomes limit choices in housing, quality of food, variety of resources, and family opportunities. Statistics show that 90 percent of the single parent households are female-headed (U.S. Bureau of Census, 1985). Single mothers face greater economic problems than single fathers because they have less psychological, educational, or occupational preparation to assume responsibilities as heads of household (Brooks, 1985; Weiss, 1984; Colletta, 1983).

Separation and divorce have immediate economic impact creating tremendous change for both parents and children. However, one needs to look more closely at what actually occurs to the single mother.

Economic Adjustments

The economic situation is quite different for mother- as compared to father-headed households. Often the father is accustomed to the role as the head prior to the divorce and is familiar with the responsibilities of the work world, the schedule, and the pace, whereas the woman is frequently overwhelmed with the world of work. This is particularly true if she has been home with the children for a number of years.

The finances in the female household are frequently strained. Alimony and child support payments are minimal contributions to the income of the home and not sufficient in any degree to support a family. Research has shown that, following a divorce, the woman's income and standard of living drastically decrease, whereas the husband's income markedly increases, as does his amount of free time and flexibility. Generally, he no longer bears the immediate responsibility of the children and can devote more time and energy to pursuing a career. What this involves for the man may be a substantial increase in salary, a promotion, or even additional leisure time.

Other studies have shown that, following a marital disruption, families at different income levels rely on different income sources. Households at the higher income level relied on earnings of the new household head, alimony, and child support. Households in the lower income category relied less on earnings of members of the household and more on public assistance. This finding increased even more after five years (Weiss, 1984).

The dependence on public assistance is devastating for thousands of single mothers. Research has shown low self-esteem when the mother is relying on outside income and assistance. The feeling of independence and control of life is fragmented by this economic dependence. The reduction of income in single parent households is met by similar reductions in food and housing costs. Cagle and Deutscher (1964) compared the yearly per capita income of families living in a housing project and found that for two parent families, the income was nearly twice as great when compared to one parent families.

The implications for the single parent household are many. For many single mothers, this reduction in income and a virtual poverty level means selecting housing in an area that is less than desirable. For others, it may involve living with a roommate or taking in boarders within the home. For a great number of single mothers, it involves frequent moves depending upon the stability of a job and employment possibilities.

The Social Status of the Single Parent Mother

Generally, women have little psychological support following separation or divorce. Frequently, they lack the financial independence to engage or initiate other social contacts. They are limited by the financial constraints of raising a child, and a satisfying social life is always a step beyond their grasp. Research has shown that single mothers are less frequently invited to parties and social functions than single fathers (Brooks, 1985).

Many single mothers find that old relationships are strained, friendships frequently dissolve, and familiar ties break down (Brooks, 1985). Many single mothers find that the single life is somewhat uncomfortable, for it involves taking risks. These include going out and initiating new friendships, exploring new areas, and trying out new activities. Frequently, these must be done alone. This is threatening to the individual who has been married for a certain length of time or is accustomed to sharing many activities and experiences with a spouse. The new situation creates even greater psychological anxiety if the marriage was an extremely intimate one over a period of years.

In addition to the threat of new activities, the mother now must carve out a new social life with other adults. This involves an active social life with other adults. This requires major adjustments for the single mother, since outside contacts require a babysitter and schedule changes in meal and bed times.

Affectively, the mother must prepare her children for these changes in schedule. Frequently, a crisis period of intense emotions follows a divorce. The mother must find the inner strength and resources to cope with grief and stress. In addition to this stress, she must be responsive and communicative to the emotional strain that her children are experiencing as a result of the divorce. Frequently, she is responsible for the explanations, the invested time, and the primary task of helping her children cope emotionally. Research (Brooks, 1985) has shown that women, more than men, are less satisfied with casual contacts and desire more intimate ties. More women than men have joined support groups. Generally, women have reported a greater interest than men in an intimate relationship, significant friendships, and stability.

This feeling of isolation is increased if the once-married mother does not have close friends, relatives, or social support in her environment. Self-esteem is extremely low in the parent who is engaged in multiple responsibilities and has little, if any, support to bear the burden. Numerous organizations have developed to assist the single parent. However, many of these organizations and agencies fail to respond to parenting needs. In addition, the number of organizations and availabilities are limited.

The Children

The U.S. Bureau of Census Report in 1985 reports that at least 17 percent of all children under eighteen live in families headed by single women and only 3 percent live in families headed by single men (U.S. Bureau of Census, 1985).

As a result of the marital disruption, the children in a female-headed household usually must make several big adjustments. First, the families may have to move to less expensive accommodations in poor neighborhoods with few safe places for children to play. The child's behavior may radically change as the result of 1) lack of space in the home to play, 2) lack of safe areas in the neighborhood, 3) restricted areas to play, and 4) fewer freedoms because of the neighborhood. The mother-headed household may frequently move in an effort to improve the home. A second major adjustment may be the quality of day care or school. Often, because the mother now has to work, she must find a day care center or perhaps another school. The quality of the care or school may be poor because of her limited income. The decrease in income has also been shown to alter mothers' behavior, making them more restrictive of children playing with household possessions which the mother values and cannot afford to replace (Kriesberg, 1970). For example, if the family has to move into a small home, the children may be restricted to playing in their own bedroom, for they no longer have a playroom. Or, on the other hand, furniture, glassware, etc. take on more value since the mother cannot afford to replace the items. Where space is limited and the value of the home furnishings are an issue, more controlling language by the single parent is evident. Consequently, children may interact less positively with the parent.

Two Parents versus One

Works by Lamb (1982) and Colletta (1983) have shown accessibility to the parent to be critical for early childhood development since the parent is necessary for modeling many social behaviors. Earlier work by Bandura (1967) argued that modeling of parental behaviors had a significant impact on the young child during the early years. Unfortunately, in the single parent household, only one parent is readily available for probing questions, formation of sexual identity, and social–cognitive development.

For example, research (Lamb, 1982) has shown fathers as more active participants of rough and tumble play than mothers. In contrast, mothers have been found to show and provide more language feedback than fathers. Accessibility of the parent is critical for the child as an emotional base or retreat. The needs of the child are multiple, and the need for a significant adult in addition to the mother is evident.

The absence of the father increases the responsibilities of the mother, which reduces the quality and quantity of time with her children (Pasley and Gecas, 1982). The absence of the father limits the amount of time the mother is able to spend with the child in several ways. First, she must assume the head of house position and be the breadwinner. This involves a full-time job averaging a forty-hour work week. Employment means day care, travel time, or adjusted school schedule. Consequently, more time is devoted to primary needs of the schedule. Many women select jobs which are compatible with parenting. Unfortunately, the majority of single working mothers report high stress, limited free time, and exhaustion by the end of the work week. The lack of energy results in low tolerance and less positive interaction with the child.

In addition, father absence has been related to negative consequences in children's behavior (Kriesberg, 1970; Brandwein, Brown, and Fox, 1974). For example, for young children, those from female-headed households lack the protective quality of having a father (Herzog and Sudia, 1974; Hetherington, Cox, and Cox, 1982). On the other hand, many children who live with the father rarely grow up without a female substitute (Brooks, 1985). The modeling of many gross motor skills like baseball, soccer, and basketball is often missing in the female-headed household. Many single mothers report a lack of interest in male-dominated sports like canoeing, fishing, and bowling.

A great deal of research (Shiff, 1982) has documented the adverse social and economic effects of father absence among young children. Children's behavior may be a direct response to: 1) father absence, 2) the social attitudes related to being a child in a single parent household, 3) mother's parenting behavior, or 4) other environmental factors resulting from the divorce or separation.

Other studies (Hetherington and Cox, 1979) have shown that pre-school boys separated from fathers at an early age are most affected by his absence. If boys are older than six at the time of separation, there is less effect on the child's masculinity. For appropriate sex typing, older male models are critically needed (Lamb, 1982). The studies (Brown, 1984) have shown that boys and girls from father-absent homes have difficulty with intellectual tasks. Specifically, they have been found to score lower on math and science tests, resulting not from less ability, but from personal qualities. However, further research is critically needed in this area of study. Many studies did not control for economic or educational factors. Still other studies did not account for length of marriage, time of divorce, or the emotional stability of the couple following the divorce.

Levy-Shiff (1982) conducted a study examining the effects of father absence with children who lived in mother-headed families. Forty Israeli father-absent children were compared with 139 children from intact families. Children's behavior at home, nursery school, and in the nursery yard was observed and rated. The children measures used denoted achievement striving, attachment, social competence with peers, negative behaviors, and separation anxiety. Mothers' attitudes were measured using the Parent Attitude Research Instrument. Results showed that child rearing attitudes of female heads of household showed greater irritability and autonomy than intact family mothers. Children from mother-headed families tended to be more emotionally dependent, displayed more separation anxiety behavior, and more developmental and behavioral disturbances as compared to children from intact families (Levy-Shiff, 1982).

This is not surprising given the emotional stress evident in the crisis stage following a divorce. Even for the calmly separating couple, there is a great deal of bitterness, regret, and internal upset. Much of the coping behavior of the parent is reflected nonverbally and verbally to the child. For example, a multitude of long explanations is needed to describe the abrupt changes in life schedules. Frequently, because of the trauma associated with divorce, parents forget to explain what seems to them obvious reasons for changes and new options in their lives as a family.

Boys from mother-headed families showed more aggression and noncompliance than girls from these families. Father absence appeared more highly related to impaired development for boys and less so for girls. Mothers' child-rearing attitudes varied because of father absence. For example, their roles appeared more restrictive in their own role as head of household.

Summary

The dissolution of a marriage does not end the family. The result is an obvious and traumatic change for all members. Another change of family structure involves the increased responsibilities of the single parent. Research has documented the multiple roles of the single parent (Klein, 1973). For example, he or she must function as the comforting parent and the just authority. On the other hand, he or she must help children develop cognitive and social skills, economically provide for the family, and maintain a healthy, happy atmosphere (Gardner, 1979; Hope and Young, 1976). The multiple roles result in parental isolation, lowered self-esteem, and minimal personal satisfaction (Colletta, 1983; Weiss, 1984).

While many children do grow up in single parent homes, research has shown many positive changes. The task of parenting alone or with a spouse is a challenging one. It is one of great risk-taking, trial and error, and constant reassessment. Fortunately, parenting is a process of growth. There is no prescription, textbook, or manual that will meet the needs and questions of all parents. However, the task of parenting requires deliberate effort to examine one's needs as a family and actively problem-solve to satisfy these needs.

References

ABIDIN, R. R. *Parenting Stress Index-Manual.* Charlottesville, VA:Pediatric Psychology (1983).

BACH, G. R. "Father Fantasies and Father Typing in Father Separated Children," *Child Development,* 17:63–80 (1975).

BANE, M. "Marital Disruption and the Lives of Children," *Journal of Social Issues,* 32(1):103–117 (1976).

BLOOM, B. *Stability and Change Characteristics.* New York:Wiley (1961).

BRANDWEIN, R. A., C. A. Brown, and E. M. Fox. "Women and Children Last: The Social Situation of Divorced Others and Their Families," *Journal of Marriage and the Family,* 36:498–514 (1974).

BROOKS, J. B. *The Process of Parenting.* Mayfield Publishing Co. (1985).

CAGLE, L. T. and I. Deutscher. "Social Mobility and Low Income Fatherless Families," paper presented at Society for the Study of Social Problems, Montreal, Quebec (1964).

COCORAN, M. E. "The Economic Consequences of Marital Dissolution for Women in the Middle Years," *Sex Roles,* 5:343–353 (1979).

COLLETTA, N. "Stressful Lives: The Situation of Divorced Mothers and Their Children," *Journal of Divorce,* 6(3):19–31 (1983).

CORNELIUS, G. M. "Children's Imaginative and Social Play in Relation to Family Structure, Maternal Stress and Attitude," Doctoral Dissertation (1986).

DUNCAN, G. J. and J. N. Morgan. *Five Thousand American Families: Patterns of Economic Progress* (vol. 4). Ann Arbor, MI:University of Michigan, Institute for Social Research (1975).

FULLER, M. "Teachers' Perceptions of Parents from Intact and Single Parent Families," *Educational Horizons* (Spring, 1982).

GLICK, P. C. and A. J. Norton. "Marrying, Divorcing and Living Together in the U.S. Today," *Population Bulletin,* 32(5) (1979).

HARTUP, W. W. "Perspectives on Child and Family Interaction: Past, Present and Future," in *Child Influences on Marital and Family Interaction,* R. M. Lerner and G. B. Spanier, eds., New York:Academic Press (1978).

HETHERINGTON, E., M. Cox, and R. Cox. "Effects of Divorce on Parents and Children in Non-traditional Families" in *Parenting and Child Development,* M. E. Lamb, ed., Lawrence Erlbaum Associates, Inc. (1982).

LAMB, M. E. *Nontraditional Families: Parenting and Child Development.* Lawrence Erlbaum Associates, Inc. (1982).

LEMASTERS, M. M. and J. DeFrain. *Parenting in Contemporary America* (4th ed.). Homewood, IL:Dorsey Press (1983).

LEWIS, M. and M. Weinraub. "The Fathers' Role in the Child's Social Network," in M. Lamb, ed., *The Role of the Father in Child Development* (1976).

PASLEY, K. and V. Gecas. "Stresses and Satisfaction of the Parental Role," *Personnel & Guidance Journal,* 62(7):400–404 (1984).

ROSSI, A. "Transition to Parenthood," *Journal of Marriage and the Family,* 30:26–39 (1969).

SCHORR, A. and P. Moen. "The Single Parent and Public Policy," *Social Policy,* 9(5):15–21 (1979).

SPEILBERGER, C. D., R. Gorsuch, and R. Lushene. *STAI Manual.* Palo Alto, CA:Consulting Psychologist (1970).

WALLERSTEIN, J. "Children of Divorce: Stress and Developmental Tasks," in *Stress, Coping and Development in Children*, McGraw-Hill Book Co. (1983).

WEISS, R. S. "The Impact of Marital Dissolution on Income and Consumption in Single-Parent Households," *Journal of Marriage and the Family*, April:115–127 (1984).

PART II

Addressing Needs:
Personal, Social, Intellectual,
and Language

IN THE SECOND part of the book, we focus on addressing pertinent needs of the parent and children in single parent families. First, Peggy E. Nadenichek addresses stress and focuses on coping strategies in "Understanding Stressors and Coping Strategies in Single Parent Families." Georgianna M. Cornelius in her contribution examines further stressing and coping mechanisms as an aspect of mental hygiene of the adult in single parent families. Next, Suzanne Kasper Getz explores parent–child relationships in "The Single Parent Family: Impact on Parent–Child Relationship." Fourth, Martha J. Lally and Susan L. Trostle describe problem areas of learning in their chapter, "Addressing Special Learning Needs of Single Parent Children." Finally, Susan L. Trostle and Francis J. Di Vesta synthesize literature on the growth of the child in their chapter, "Language and Social Development of the Child from the Single Parent Family."

The major concepts that integrate and link these chapters together are: (a) stress factors and coping strategies, (b) parent–child relations, (c) children's learning needs, and (d) children's language and social growth. Each of these concepts is explained in the following sections.

Stress Factors and Coping Strategies

Nadenichek and Cornelius, in their respective chapters, examine various approaches in understanding stressors and stress factors in family settings. Most approaches to understanding and coping with stress in family units view stress and coping as a series of phases, levels, or events with marked beginning and ending points. The beginning point in the majority of these approaches usually marks the onset, causal factors, or sources of problems, and the ending point, the conceptual adaptation and integration of them in which family members come to understand and work with them in meaningful ways. However, the terminating point in the majority of these approaches is usually viewed as a long-range effort by involved family members to try to conceptualize and in turn recover from the crises. This long-range effort can span years. The levels or phases between the beginning and ending of the crises describe the individual family members' definitions and understandings of the crises and the identification of family resources that could be used to meet them. Across all levels or phases, these various approaches to understanding and coping with stress also account for ongoing conceptual adaptation and the amount of disorganization in the family unit that is produced by it. In addition, these various approaches also take into consideration related life stressors and changes influencing the family's capacity to achieve varying degrees of adaptation and the processes the family uses to achieve resolution. Understanding these approaches to family crises provides a systematic framework to reestablishing family adaptation.

Common to these various approaches is the initial event or series of events that taken together may have triggered the crisis. Within the context of the single parent family, there are numerous stressors that impinge on the family unit. These problems or stressors as noted by Nadenichek and related ones by Cornelius include: (a) selected pragmatic issues, (b) interpersonal and social problems, (c) family-related stress, and (d) emotional reactions.

Briefly, stressors related to selected pragmatic issues include those related to household management, home maintenance and finances. Interpersonal and social problems, as stressors, focus on the shifting of friends which usually occurs when adults move from intact to single parent families. This reestablishing of interpersonal relationships greatly assists the single parent in his or her ability to cope successfully with social needs. Factors related to family-generated stress focus on roles and boundaries of family units; when separation and divorce occur, the roles and boundaries become ambiguous. This situation occurs, in part, because of pressures from extended family members on the divorced adults, as well as the changing demands of the adults in single parent families (e.g., need for more autonomy). Stressors pertinent to emotional reactions arise during and after divorce as basic reactions and actions to this situation. Several of these may include low self-esteem, depression, anger, and hopelessness.

Within and as a response to stressors and the need for adults to readapt to changing family situations, Nadenichek and Cornelius discuss several coping strategies that contribute to the readjustment processes. Briefly, decision making as a coping strategy to stressors requires the single parent to develop new goals, routines, and new standards and roles. In addition, successful coping strategies include the establishment and refinement of social networks set within formal and informal resources that can be marshalled to assist the readaptation of the single parent.

In sum, the degree to which the single parent recovers from divorce situations is directly related to the understanding of the stressors and development and use of coping strategies. And, the stressors and coping mechanisms are viewed within one of many approaches as a workable framework for readjusting and readapting to changes in life and family situations.

Parent–Child Relations

Getz recognizes that the single parent family directly and indirectly impacts the relationships between parent and child. From the beginning of the problems brought on by divorce to readaptation, family members readjust to find a new "well-being." This new well-being involves reestablishing parent–child relationships. In this regard, Getz notes that parent–child relationships benefit if children's questions of well-being and those related to coping are addressed.

Developing constructive and genuine parent–child relations, according to Getz, means the single parent and child must attend to: (a) realities of divorce, (b) development of functional team members within the single parent family, (c) everyday relations between parent and child, and (d) personal development of each individual.

First, recognizing the realities of divorce contributes to establishing meaningful parent and child relationships. Recognizing divorce means understanding that the family unit is legally dissolved. Recognizing the dissolution as a legal situation rather than placing blame on an individual parent helps establish constructive parent-child relations. Children's questions about the divorce should be answered in a meaningful and genuine way. These questions usually focus on the time, place, and cause of the divorce. In recognizing the realities of divorce, Getz feels that the feelings of children should not be overlooked or ignored. These feelings include the fact that the children miss the other adult in the family and will want to be with him or her. This is a special time to understand these feelings as an approach to the well-being of the family. Involved with feelings are liabilities of the children toward both adults. Children also experience fears about themselves and others as they recognize the realities of divorce. Developing child–parent relationships in these situations means helping the child understand fears and answering questions about protection with many examples and in meaningful contexts.

In addition to working through fears, developing strong parent–child relationships is dependent on developing and carrying out details for children's and parent's visits and establishing appropriate behaviors in the two households. For consistency between households and furthering of child–parent relationships, the parent who remains in and the one who leaves the family unit should agree on behaviors and child guidance standards which should be maintained within each of the households.

Basic to child–parent relationships is the need for both parents living in different households to maintain their integrity and especially the integrity of the absent parent. Finally, the reality of divorce has impacts beyond the family, such as with relatives and neighbors. In establishing parent–child relationships, children should be prepared for these impacts as much as possible. Letting the children know that relatives and neighbors may have questions concerning the divorce and providing the children with genuine and truthful answers will not only prepare them for these situations, but will also help them develop meaningful parent–child relationships.

The second major factor that helps develop parent–child relationships is helping the child and other family members function as team members of the family. This shift in roles from the adult as executive and "decider" to one of team member is necessary if the members of the family are to function as team members. Here, decision making and problem solving concerning pertinent family issues are shared with children on those issues where the adult really desires team functioning. This team membership perspective can occur within a family unit regardless of the ages of the children—from preschoolers to adolescents. The team approach to family functioning which Getz emphasizes can minimize family disruptions and deal effectively with times of stress.

The third major factor that helps develop parent–child relationships is the single parent's attempt to nurture continually these relations as a part of ongoing socialization processes. For example, by modelling, the single parent can show trust, open communication, and positive guidance in daily activities and actions. Simply by demonstrating these traits with children and adolescents, parent and child relationships can be nurtured effectively. Getz asserts that continuing to nurture parent–child relationships not only develops a strong family unit but also prepares children and adolescents for adulthood.

Finally, parent–child relationships can also be developed as part of the personal growth of each individual. Maximizing personal development of each individual in the family unit means viewing the parent as a parent to the child and an adult among adults, as well as viewing the child as a child to the parent and a child among children. From this viewpoint, the personal development of each person as an individual is stressed. In similar manner, each individual becomes a member of several groups whose roles change as a function of membership in these groups. It is imperative in child–parent relationships that emphasis be given to personal development. By maximizing these "out-of-house" interests and responsibilities, coping strategies and greater respect for the individual evolve.

In sum, parent–child relations are severely impacted through divorce. Constructive ways of strengthening these relationships among members within the single parent family, as well as between the child and the adult who has left the household, help maximize family and individual growth, ameliorate stresses, and prepare for readaptation and readjustment of family members.

Children's Learning Needs

Lally and Trostle address special learning needs of single parent children by exploring various aspects including dealing with emotional reactions and various interventions at home: those with adolescents, those that are more social, and others that are school based.

In a practical sense, Lally and Trostle point out that the emotional reactions experienced by single parents of learning-needs children include self-blame, loss of self-control, confusion, and intolerance. Like parents of intact families, single parent heads of household feel partially responsible for the learning need. However, their self-blame may be greater because they assume the majority of self-blame and "shoulder" these feelings. In addition, the single parent may blame or feel hostility toward the other parent living outside the house of learning-needs children. Loss of self-control, confusion, and intolerance are related emotional feelings that adults in single parent families may show about their learning-needs children.

Regardless of the feelings and emotional reactions of the parent, there are several effective approaches that single parents may use in dealing with their children with learning problems. Home intervention is a possible approach discussed by Lally and Trostle. Home intervention approaches as strategies cover development of self-awareness and especially working with children in motor, listening, and language development. As a segment of home intervention, older children may need to understand the importance of limit-setting, chores, and play.

Intervening with adolescents as an approach of single parents with learning-needs children involves a differing set of routines. In a practical sense, dealing with household planning, managing money and others such as choosing a career are of paramount importance. Lally and Trostle stress that adolescents need to learn to make decisions for themselves. Some of these routine decisions involve clothing purchases and food selection at restaurants. Single parent families need to help their adolescents with special learning needs and focus on their areas of strength.

On another plane, intervention is social intervention. Because children with learning needs exhibit problems in social relationships, special efforts need to be made by the single parent in this growth area. These special efforts include interpreting the child's statements to others and determining the amount of different situations he can tolerate at any one encounter. There is also psychological intervention which attempts to develop a healthy self-concept in the learning-needs child. Selected strategies identified by Lally and Trostle include learning from the child and giving extra reassurance for accomplishments.

In addition, Lally and Trostle stress school intervention as another viable form of attempting to help single parents work with their learning-needs child. Areas to explore here include school readiness and behavior problems in classroom settings. Lastly, there is professional involvement with guidance counselors, teachers, nurses, and others. These professionals provide extended forms of assistance and can do a great deal to enhance the effectiveness and ease the strain often experienced by single parents with learning-needs children.

These approaches and special forms of intervention help parents in single parent families to cope with and facilitate growth of their special-needs child. As a group they focus on three dimensions of assistance to the single parent family: cognitive, affective, and psychomotor.

Children's Language and Social Growth

Trostle and Di Vesta address the language and social development of children from single parent families. Research literature, in general, shows that language, social, and cognitive development are complexly intertwined. Adult–child and child–child interaction is an especially vital area where those various levels of growth become integrated. The primary sources of early contacts are provided by the adult and siblings. The kinds of terms used as labels for objects, length of nurturances, and cognitive content all provide baselines for language and social growth of the child in single parent families. Within adult–child interaction, the single parent may wish to use recastings of utterances with integrate the child's readiness and challenge his linguistic level. An example of recasting is where a child notes that, "It broke." The single parent in turn recasts the sentence by saying, for example, "The cup fell from the table and broke."

Since the roles of language and social skills are interactive, Trostle and Di Vesta point out several needs of children from single parent families if they are to reach their full potential. Among them are the child's ability to interact and his or her motivation. Not only must the child have the language capacity, but he must have a receptive social climate in which to interact.

In addition, Trostle and Di Vesta address the effect of gender of the single parent on the child's language and social development. Although the research is very limited, there seems to be some agreement that girls, rather than boys, living with their fathers in single parent families may have more problems in language and social development. In addition, research findings (e.g., Santrock, Warshak, and Elliott, 1982) show that girls living in mother-headed single parent families may show more competent social behavior than girls in stepfather families. Moreover, children from single parent families appear to require teacher and parent encouragement in order for them to strike a better balance in the roles of "traditional" girl and boy.

In a final note, Trostle and Di Vesta emphasize language and social growth factors related to children's play. The chief motivating factor for promoting language development is intrinsic. And, play is self-generated and oriented towards children's own goals. Play becomes an ideal medium for communication. In this regard, the single parent needs to provide a stimulating play environment that challenges the children's assuming leadership and asking relevant questions.

Emphasizing and promoting child's language and social skills is of primary importance for the single parent. By providing a model for child–parent interaction and using strategies such as recasting, children from single parent families can develop constructive communication patterns. In addition, the child's participation in play is also another way for children to grow in language and social development.

Conclusion

Children from both intact and single parent families have needs and require guidance from the adult(s) to develop as members of the family unit and as individuals. However, children and parents from single parent families may need greater attention to specific growth areas by the single parent and competent professionals.

In initially addressing these needs, the single parent should understand the stressors that can create problems within a single parent family. These include financial concerns and the adaptation cycle for adjusting to a divorce. Moreover, the single parent will need to develop and use coping strategies in order to deal effectively with these stressors.

After understanding stressors and coping strategies, examining parent–child relationships is effective in redeveloping the family unit. If the parent in the single parent family has children with special needs, ways of working and intervening are necessary for the parent as well as the child. And, regardless of the degree of special need, the parent of children within a single parent family can encourage and nurture language and social growth of the children. By addressing pertinent personal, social, intellectual, and language needs, the adult in the single parent family can better assist the children as individuals, the family as the unit, and himself/herself as the parent.

Reference

SANTROCK, J. W., R. A. Warshak, and G. L. Elliott, ''Social Development and Parent–Children Interaction in Father-Custody and Stepmother Families,'' in *Nontraditional Families: Parenting and Child Development*, M. E. Lamb, ed., Hillsdale, NJ:Lawrence Erlbaum Associates, Inc. (1982).

Understanding Stressors and Coping Strategies in Single Parent Families

PEGGY E. NADENICHEK

Introduction

IDENTIFYING STRESSORS AND the need to cope with them is a common theme throughout society today. Workshops, conferences, classes, books, and research are educating the public on how to manage stress and live healthy, relaxing, longer lives.

Stress affects individuals and systems. It results from normative events (getting married, parenting, moving to a new home, changing jobs, divorce), as well as events that are not considered normative (war, fire, unemployment, death, illness, accidents, natural disasters) (McCubbin and Figley, 1983).

In contemporary society, divorce is receiving increasing attention as normative. It is also a phenomenon that is stress-inducing and affects millions of adults and children annually. Increasing numbers of single parent families are required to adjust and adapt to demands and stressors facing each family member as a result of separation or divorce (Hogan, Buehler, and Robinson, 1983).

Theoretical and practical approaches for understanding stress in single parent families are presented in this chapter. Since marital dissolution is the major cause of single parent families (Hogan et al., 1983), this chapter focuses mainly on single parent families that have resulted from divorce or separation. First, conceptual frameworks (Hill, 1958; McCubbin and Patterson, 1983a) for viewing families under stress are defined. Second, research findings on stressors and coping mechanisms of single parent families are discussed. Third, the theoretical frameworks and research findings are applied to case studies of single parent families.

39

The ABCX Models of Family Crisis

The Original ABCX Model

Hill's (1958) original model emerged from the field of sociology (McCubbin and Patterson, 1983a). It is a simple configuration showing why families differ in their definitions, coping strategies, and adaptations to family stress and crisis. The model is composed of the following elements: "A (the event) → interacting with B (the family's crisis-meeting resources) → *interacting* with C (the definition the family makes of the event) → *produces* X (the crisis)" (Hill, 1958, p. 141). In order to explain crisis-proneness in families, it is possible to examine the elements separately and identify variables which cause stress and lead to family crises.

The Event (A Factor)

The event which occurs at the onset is seen as stressful and has the potential to produce demands or changes on the family social system (McCubbin and Patterson, 1983a). Hill (1958) describes a classification of stressor events which includes three systems to catalog crises: (a) by source of trouble, whether inside or outside the family; (b) by effects on the family configuration, whether it involves the loss of a family member (dismemberment), the addition of a family member (accession), and/or the loss of family morale and unity (demoralization); and (c) the type of event which could be a sudden change in family status or conflict among family members regarding their roles.

Crisis-Meeting Resources (B Factor)

Burr (1973) describes family resources for meeting stressful demands or changes as the ability of a family to prevent the event from creating a crisis or disruption. Family sociologist, Robert Angell (1936), identifies two concepts which explain family resources—family integration and family adaptability. Family integration refers to coherence and unity within family life, emphasizing common interests, affection, and economic interdependence (Angell, 1936). Family adaptability includes the capacity to meet obstacles and shift courses of action as a family.

Other family theorists describe additional resources. Cavan and Ranck (1938) and Koos (1946) look at adequate and inadequate family organization. The quality of organization depends on: (a) the family's agreement about its role structure, (b) its satisfaction in meeting physical and emotional needs of the family members, (c) subordination of personal ambitions to family goals, and (d) goals the family members work toward together.

Family Definition of the Event (C Factor)

The family's subject definition of the stressor explains the C factor in the ABCX Model. Subjective meanings reflect the family's values and previous experience in dealing with crises (Hill, 1958). A family's meaning of a crisis-provoking event can range from viewing it as a challenge to the other extreme of seeing it as an uncontrollable event.

Family Crisis (X Factor)

Burr (1973) conceptualizes crisis as a continuous variable that characterizes the amount of disruptiveness, disorganization, or incapacitation in the family structure. Stressful events or life transitions that cause disruption require coping mechanisms to correct subsequent imbalance in the family system. When the family is able to restore stability by using existing resources, the stress may never reach crisis proportions. Conversely, if the family does not adequately meet the demands of the situation, stress may reach a crisis state (McCubbin and Patterson 1983a). Figure 3.1 (Hill, 1958, p. 145) depicts interaction between a stressful event and family resources in producing a crisis.

Post-Crisis Behaviors

Hill's (1958) ABCX Model examines precrisis variables or the potential for crisis. Depending on the degree to which a family crisis has been resolved, it may be necessary to examine post-crisis variables or the long-range efforts a family uses to recover from a crisis.

An expansion of the original ABCX Model (Hill, 1958) has emerged from studies of family crises induced by war (McCubbin, Boxx, Wilson, and Lester, 1980; McCubbin and Patterson, 1981, 1982, 1983a, 1983b). The expanded model, known as the Double ABCX Model, is diagrammed in Figure 3.2 (McCubbin and Patterson, 1983a, p. 12).

The Double ABCX Model

As depicted in Figure 3.2, the factors in the double model are similar to those in the original model. The expansion is "an effort to describe: (a) the additional life stressors and changes which may influence the family's ability to achieve adaptation; (b) the critical psychological and social factors families call upon and use in manag-

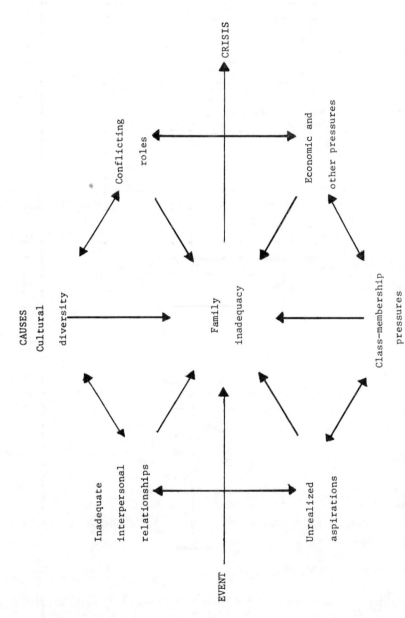

FIGURE 3.1. Diagram showing the interaction of stressor event, contributing hardships, and family resources in producing a family crisis.

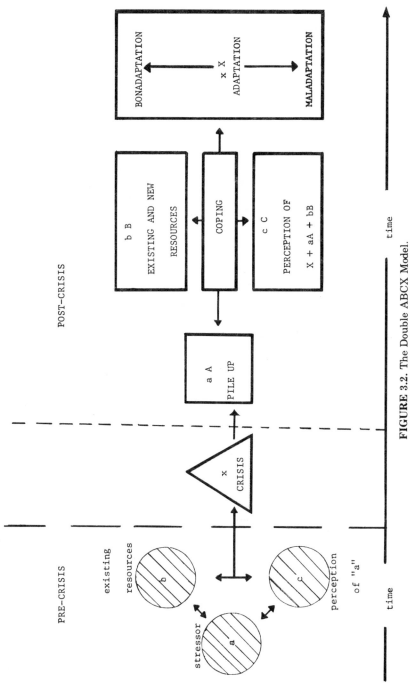

FIGURE 3.2. The Double ABCX Model.

ing crisis situations; (c) the processes families engage in to achieve satisfactory resolution; and (d) the outcome of these family efforts" (McCubbin and Patterson, 1983a, p. 11).

Pile-up of Demands (aA Factor)

Stressful events rarely occur in isolation. More often, families deal with multiple stressors simultaneously. McCubbin and Patterson (1983a) categorize five general types of stressors which contribute to pile up during a family crisis:

(1) *Stressor and its hardships.* Any changing event, whether it is divorce, career change, or the addition of a new member to the family unit, produces other needs and stressors that a family needs to contend with.

(2) *Normative transitions.* In addition to the major transition resulting from the original crisis, normal growth and developmental transitions occur across individuals and families.

(3) *Prior strains.* Individuals and families carry unresolved issues with them which tend to resurface or exacerbate when a new stressor is introduced.

(4) *Consequences of family efforts to cope.* When a family does attempt to deal with a crisis situation, additional stressors may result from the coping mechanisms or behaviors the family uses.

(5) *Intrafamily and social ambiguity.* When change occurs, there is some uncertainty and ambiguity about the future. Family systems experience additional stress if they are unsure of which members are physically and psychologically inside and outside the system boundaries (Boss, 1977, 1980).

Similarly, ambiguity can occur at the social level, given unclear guidelines established by culture, society, or community when dealing with families under stress.

Adaptive Resources (bB Factor)

Resources are necessary for meeting the demands in many facets of life. When a family is faced with a stressful or crisis-producing situation, resources are of primary importance for meeting needs which arise. McCubbin and Patterson (1983a) classify resources as: (a) personal, (b) social support, and (c) family system resources.

Personal resources include finances, education (enhancing realistic stress perception and problem-solving skills), health (physical and emotional), and psychological resources. Pearlin and Schooler

(1978) identify self-esteem (positiveness of one's self-attitude) and mastery (perceived control over one's life) as important personal psychological resources.

Social support describes a family's interpersonal level and includes: (a) emotional support (belief by family unit or members that they are cared for or loved); (b) esteem support (family unit or members feeling esteemed and valued; and (c) network support (members or family unit sensing mutual obligation and understanding from neighbors, friends, relatives, self-help groups, or community agencies).

Family system resources describe the degree to which a family functions with cohesion (integration) and adaptability. Too much cohesion creates enmeshment, while too little cohesion leads to disengagement of family members. Similarly, a family system can become chaotic from too much adaptability and rigid from too little adaptability. Therefore, moderate functioning on both dimensions results in more successful adaptation to crises (Olson and McCubbin, 1982).

Family Definition and Perception (cC Factor)

As in Hill's (1958) original ABCX Model, if a family is able to redefine the stressful situation as a challenge or an opportunity for positive change, the chances of successful adjustment and adaptation increase. Effective problem solving and emphasis on appropriate social and emotional development are important factors the family must work towards (McCubbin and Patterson, 1983a).

Family Adaptation (xX Factor)

In the Double ABCX Model (McCubbin and Patterson, 1983a), reciprocal relationships between demands and capabilities are analyzed between: (a) individual family members and the family unit and (b) the family unit and the community of which the family is a part. Adaptation occurs when the demands of one unit are met by the capabilities of the other. Conversely, family stress may occur when there is a demand–capability imbalance. When seeking balance, both levels of family functioning need to be recognized since a change in one level affects the other level (McCubbin and Patterson, 1983a).

Family adaptation occurs across a continuum. McCubbin and Patterson (1983a) call the positive end of the continuum *bonadaptation* and the negative end *maladaptation*. A family could be anywhere along the continuum based on the family's demands, resources, and perception of the situation.

Profile of Single Parent Families

Stressors of Single Parent Families

The transition a family experiences from separation or divorce rarely occurs without related stress or demands on the family members or unit. The majority of single parent families experience a pile-up of stressors described theoretically in the Double ABCX Model. Even after a certain adjustment period, single parent families experience a set of demands that differs from those of dual parent families.

It was common prior to the 1960s to emphasize the effects of single parenting on the children (Schlesinger, 1966). Gradually, the emphasis shifted from children to custodial parent, with the belief that parental adjustment strongly affects children's adjustment (Gasser and Taylor, 1976). Recently, literature, school support groups, and community services began focusing on helping children cope with the divorce or separation of their parents (Taylor, 1982).

The theoretical models of family crisis discussed earlier and the research that follows assume that single parent family adjustment is largely a function of parental issues. This does not deny that children need to understand divorce and learn to cope with the subsequent stress, but it places the major responsibility for the quality of crisis resolution on the parents.

Recent research describes four major categories of problems and stressors experienced by single parents: (a) pragmatic issues, (b) interpersonal and social problems, (c) family-related stress, and (d) emotional reactions (Bloom, Asher, and White, 1978; Hetherington, Cox, and Cox, 1976; Levinger, 1976).

Pragmatic Issues

Single mothers (Bohannon, 1970; Brandwein, Brown, and Fox, 1974; Epenshade, 1979; Glasser and Navarre, 1965; Yates, 1976) and single fathers (Gasser and Taylor, 1976; Mendes, 1976; Orthner, Brown, and Ferguson, 1976; Victor and Winkler, 1977) encounter difficulties in the areas of household management, finances, home and employment coordination, and home maintenance. Responsibilities once shared by both parents to some degree are now assumed by one parent and sometimes shared with the children. Generally, single parents feel overwhelmed by the constant demands placed on them, finding enough time to do everything, and knowing how to do it (Berman and Turk, 1981; Colletta, 1983).

As the roles of men and women become less stereotyped in today's society (Hogan et al., 1983), single fathers have become more capable of making the necessary adjustments in practical areas that were traditionally the mother's responsibility (Smith and Smith, 1981). Single fathers see their new role as a challenge and an opportunity to prove to society that they are adequate parents although gaps exist in society's preparation and expectations for fatherhood (Gasser and Taylor, 1976; Mendes, 1976; Smith and Smith, 1981). Hetherington, Cox, and Cox (1978) suggest that single mothers have more difficulty handling their children after marital dissolution even though traditionally they assumed major child care responsibilities during marriage. Santrock and Warshak (1979) report no difference in parenting competency between single mothers and fathers. Rather, successful single parenthood appears to reflect personal understanding and goals as much as task familiarity and behavioral preparation (Wedemeyer and Johnson, 1982).

Economic resources are more of a constraint for single mothers than for single fathers (Espenshade, 1979) although this is changing as reflected by changes in the work force (Pichitino, 1983). Traditionally, women have not been the main breadwinners in most families (Wedemeyer and Johnson, 1982), but after marital dissolution, the majority of single mothers assume this role (Brandwein, 1977; Weiss, 1984). Single mothers usually experience a decrease in income sources after divorce (Weiss, 1984) and earn less income than single fathers (Keith and Schafer, 1982; Pichitino, 1983). Although single fathers seldom report a significant loss of income during the transition to single fatherhood (Smith and Smith, 1981), Ferri (1973) and Spanier and Casto (1979) note that some single fathers do experience a decrease in income.

Overall, sex role orientation plays an important part in single mothers' adjustment to economic, home, and child care changes. Keith and Schafer (1982) show that single working mothers who maintain traditional male– female roles may experience more adjustment problems than single working mothers who are not traditional in their outlook on provider roles and housekeeping, regardless of income. Similarly, Brown and Manela (1978) associate nontraditional sex role attitudes in women with lower distress regardless of employment status or education.

Interpersonal and Social Problems

Most single parents experience stress associated with their social life and in establishing meaningful interpersonal relationships. The transition to single parenthood is generally accompanied by a shift to friends who are single (Gasser and Taylor, 1976; Hetherington et al., 1976; Pichitino, 1983; Smith and Smith, 1981). Gasser and Taylor (1976) report that single fathers discontinued memberships in social groups and clubs due to increasing demands at home or feeling out of place after becoming single. Social life for single parents tends to decline initially, then increase after divorce or separation (Hetherington et al., 1976). Since the shift to single social participant is stressful, single parents need to establish a social network of friends and family (Kayak and Linney, 1983).

Society has no clear models or established cultural patterns to follow on single parenting (McCubbin and Patterson, 1983a; Mendes, 1976; Pichitino, 1983), possibly creating prejudices and ambivalent attitudes by relatives, friends, or neighbors towards single parents (Brandwein et al., 1974; Miller, 1970; Smith and Smith, 1981). Some religions discourage or do not recognize divorce; single women are stereotyped as threats to marriages and single men are characterized as playboys; married couples are unsure of how to maintain friendships with divorced friends. Men often aren't willing to become involved with single women who have children (Goode, 1956). These issues create stress and role conflict when interpersonal and social needs arise.

Family-Related Stress

Roles for family members (Hogan et al., 1983; McCubbin and Patterson, 1983a) and boundaries of family systems (Boss, 1977) become ambiguous when a marriage breaks up. Family members have to negotiate in order to redefine household responsibilities and carry out tasks normally performed by the absent spouse (Hogan et al., 1983). Periods of conflict occur between ex-spouses regarding finances, visitation, child rearing, and intimate relations with others; attachments occasionally occur interspersed with anger and resentment (Hetherington et al., 1976; Weiss, 1975, 1976). Depending on the ex-spouses' relationship, plus the extended family members' perceptions of divorce, ties with relatives may become strained (Hogan et al., 1983; McCubbin and Patterson, 1983a).

Interactions between parents and children change after divorce or separation. Hetherington et al. (1976) report initially that single parents "make fewer maturity demands of their children, communicate less well with their children, tend to be less affectionate with their children and show marked inconsistency in discipline and lack of control over their children in comparison to parents in intact families" (p. 424). As several years pass, mothers demand more autonomous, mature behavior, communicate better, are more consistent and nurturant, and control their children better (Hetherington et al., 1976). Orthner et al. (1976) found that single fathers feel they do not have enough time for their children, lack patience with them, and demand more independence in them than other parents do although they report a close and affectionate relationship with their children. Single fathers with daughters express concern over their daughters' sexuality, sexual behavior, and lack of female role model (Mendes, 1976). The parent–child relationships tend to restabilize sooner when ex-spouses agree on child rearing and disciplining of the children when visitation is involved (Hetherington et al., 1976).

Emotional Reactions

During and after a divorce or separation, family members experience emotional problems (Berman and Turk, 1981) including low self-esteem, depression, confusion over role changes, and feelings of anger, hopelessness, and less behavior control (Berman and Turk, 1981; Pett, 1981). Emotions influence and are influenced by the other problem areas which single parents face. Therefore, Berman and Turk (1981), Chiriboga, Coho, Stein, and Roberts (1979), McLanahan (1976), and Pett (1982) stress the importance of the availability and use of interpersonal resources when coping with emotional problems resulting from the transition to single parenthood.

Coping Mechanisms Used in Single Parent Families

When a family is confronted with demands created by a crisis event, the members may employ adjustment coping strategies and then make efforts towards adaptation. Adjustment strategies in the form of avoidance, elimination, and/or assimilation create the least amount of disruption in the family's behavior pattern (McCubbin and Patterson, 1983a). Avoidance involves the family's attempts to deny the stressors in the hope that they will resolve themselves; elimination is an effort to change the stressor or alter its definition; and assimilation involves the family accepting the stressor and making minor changes within the family's structure. When the crisis is precipitated by divorce or separation, a structural change has already occurred in the family unit and adjustment strategies are insufficient to meet the demands created by the transition to single parenthood.

Adaptation requires the family to make additional changes in their existing structure. Buehler and Hogan (1980) propose that single parent families implement new management behavior, including: "(a) setting new goals, (b) adjusting the level and standard of living, (c) exploring new resources and reorganizing routines to maximize resource effectiveness, and (d) redefining role expectations and negotiating task performance responsibilities" (p. 520).

Decision Making

In attempts to reduce family stress by creating new goals and routines and establishing new rules, standards, and roles, appropriate decision making is essential (Buehler and Hogan, 1980; Paolucci, Hall, and Axinn, 1977). Family members need the knowledge and ability to generate alternative courses of action and weigh the consequences in order to make adequate short-term and long-term decisions regarding crucial issues. If a family is operating on a high stress level, the need to make daily survival decisions may lower its level of functioning. It then becomes difficult to set new goals and standards and change roles. The more willing a parent is to reassess the family's resources, establish a new sex-role identity, and change the family standard of living, the more adaptable the stress becomes (Hogan et al., 1983).

A family can move towards improved management by making small incremental changes or by implementing a long-range comprehensive plan (Buehler and Hogan, 1980). Types of incremental changes vary. For example, children may assume more household responsibilities; a parent may work overtime or borrow money for expenses; household budgeting may become tighter; friends, neighbors, or relatives may help with child care, household maintenance, or financial support. For a family with numerous major stressors and demands, a comprehensive program is the more effective plan of action. This involves a combination of incremental steps, as well as the possibility of a complete career change and/or a geographic relocation. An incremental plan may develop into a comprehensive plan. In either case, along with appropriate decision making, the use of a social network facilitates adaptation.

Social Networks

A social network consists of informal and formal resources. Informal resources make use of relatives, neighbors, friends, co-workers, and other acquaintances. Formal resources are those which involve professional intervention.

Families have a tendency to obtain help from informal sources more readily than from formal sources, although this may depend on the level and type of stress being experienced. Families or individuals, in general, mention family, relatives, and friends as sources of help more frequently then clergymen, physicians, mental health centers, or other community agencies (Eddy, Paap, and Glad, 1970; Koos, 1946; Rosenblatt and Mayer, 1972; Turner, Kimbrough, and Traynhan, 1977). Divorced men and women most commonly seek assistance from friends, ex-spouses, counselors, relatives, and parents, in that order (Chiriboga et al., 1979). Single mothers who have healthy interactions with their children obtain support from sources inside and outside the family unit (Brassard, 1979). Single fathers report first contacting parents and relatives, next friends, and then professional counselors when problems arise (Orthner et al., 1976). McLanahan et al. (1981) recommend that single mothers develop support networks ranging from close-knit (maintaining family and friendship ties) to loose-knit (establishing new social contacts), depending on their role orientation—maintaining pre-divorce identity or seeking a new identity.

As indicated earlier in the chapter, there are times when support from family and friends can be ambiguous or negative (Brandwein et al., 1974; Hogan et al., 1983; McCubbin and Patterson, 1983a; Miller, 1970; Smith and Smith, 1981). Mendes (1976) notes that single fathers could obtain occasional help from relatives but are sometimes reluctant to admit they need help. Establishing intimate adult relationships may help reduce stress for single parents (Hetherington et al., 1976), but the children's reactions may be stress-producing.

A variety of community resources not yet mentioned are useful to subsidize income, help with child care, or provide informational and social contacts for single parents. Government assistance programs include such resources as food stamps, public assistance, G.I. Bill, educational loans, scholarships, public housing, and day care. Organizations such as Parents Without Partners (Orthner et al., 1976), Big Brother/Big Sister (Taylor, 1982), and local churches offer support and relief from the stress and demands facing single parents. Sometimes the stigma and instability of government assistance programs and the limitations of child care facilities create additional stress rather than provide an outlet (Bould, 1977; Colletta, 1979; Hogan et al., 1983; Orthner et al., 1976).

Proposed Educational/Counseling Model

Wedemeyer and Johnson (1982, p. 45) illustrate the application of Hill's (1958) ABCX Model to the transition from dual to single parenthood in Figure 3.3. Based on previous research and their inter-

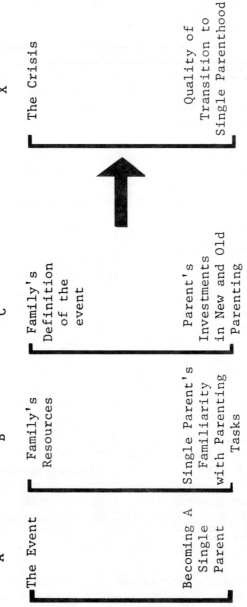

FIGURE 3.3. Application of Hill's ABCX Model of family crisis to the transition to single parenthood.

views with single parents, Wedemeyer and Johnson (1982, pp. 51–52) developed the following steps for use in educational and counseling settings:

(1) *List tasks facing the single parent* (Hill's A factor). The tasks need to be evaluated in terms of strengths and weaknesses.
(2) *List tasks carried out by each spouse while married* (Hill's B factor). Using Figure 3.4 (Wedemeyer and Johnson, 1982, p. 43) as a guide, discuss the division of labor and any imbalances that may have occurred during marriage.
(3) *Draw the relationship between the dual parent and single parent situations* (Hill's B and C factors interacting). Discuss the transition that needs to occur regarding parenting tasks and the potential of role overload.
(4) *Evaluate the single parent's level of efficiency and ego investment with current tasks* (Hill's A and C factors interacting). Explore ways to coordinate, delegate, or streamline tasks and discuss personal losses or gains that may occur with new goals and behaviors.

This model provides the steps necessary for learning adaptive decision making and helps identify potential areas where social networks can assist the single parent family.

Case Studies

The following excerpts from case studies illustrate how different families respond to the single parent transition.

(1) Tom is a thirty-one-year-old parent whose seven-year-old son came to live with him when he and his wife separated four years ago. Tom had assumed the majority of housekeeping, child rearing, and employment responsibilities prior to the separation, so it was not difficult for him to juggle the same roles as a single parent. He and his son continued to live in the same vicinity as his ex-wife and in-laws. Tom's own mother was deceased and he had minimal contact with his brothers and no contact with his father.

While living near his ex-relatives, Tom faced pressures, especially from his ex-mother-in-law, over how to raise his son. His ex-wife maintained occasional, irregular contacts with their son. Tom had to leave several jobs because of the demands at home and pressures from his ex-mother-in-law. His social life became almost nonexistent.

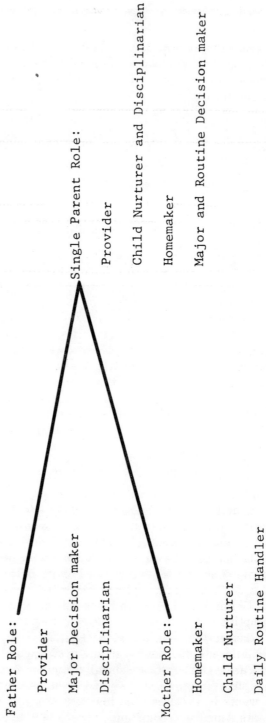

Traditional Marital Partnership:

Separation or Divorce:

Father Role:

Provider

Major Decision maker

Disciplinarian

Mother Role:

Homemaker

Child Nurturer

Daily Routine Handler

Single Parent Role:

Provider

Child Nurturer and Disciplinarian

Homemaker

Major and Routine Decision maker

FIGURE 3.4. Parental tasks and the transition to single parenthood.

Recently, Tom and his son moved to a college community 150 miles away from the ex-relatives, and Tom returned to complete a college education he had started when his son was an infant. Tom obtained financial support from G.I. benefits and Federal student loans. Since he lacks support from any family members, Tom has had to rely on new acquaintances from his apartment building for social interaction, emotional support, and occasional baby-sitting. It has been difficult for his son to adjust to a new home, new school, and less contact from his mother and other relatives.

Fortunately for Tom, his ex-mother-in-law is slowly but reluctantly releasing her sense of control over him, and his life is beginning to stabilize. He plans to involve his son in Little League and Boy Scouts, where his son will gain friendships, achievements, and structure during his free time, while Tom will become involved in more of his son's activities and have the opportunity to meet other parents. He has become friends with another single father whose daughter is around his son's age.

Even though Tom is faced with financial pressures and demands on his time, he is glad he has chosen this path and wonders why he didn't make the break sooner.

(2) Carol is a twenty-six-year-old mother with custody of her two- and four-year-old daughters. She left her husband six months ago after a history of violent arguments. She moved to a town forty miles away, enrolled her children in day care, and began to work full-time.

Carol's life changed from that of a subservient wife and overprotective mother to a single parent with a career and active social life. She feels conflict between her past role as the perfect mother and her current emphasis on career and friends. For the first time in her life, Carol is making her own decisions, but they are affecting her relationship with her children. While she is exploring her new independence, her children are spending the majority of their time at day care or with baby-sitters.

One of Carol's more responsible baby-sitters contacted the local Children and Youth Service agency after unsuccessfully attempting to convince Carol that her frustration and confusion were creating a potentially abusive situation with her children. The Children and Youth caseworker suggested Carol attend a local Parents Anonymous support group. Carol realizes that her stress stems from role conflict and she is unsure whether or not she wants to keep her children, but she will not attend the Parents Anonymous meetings, nor will she make any changes in her current level of functioning that will affect her work hours or social life. She remains in a high stress situation.

(3) Sandy is a thirty-three-year-old single mother with four children. She has been separated from her second husband for the past year. She has her four children living with her—a daughter age twelve and a son age nine from her first marriage and a daughter age one and a son age two from her second marriage. Sandy moved from a large home in a rural community to a small duplex in an urban area approximately fifteen miles away. She is not pleased with the lack of space in their home and does not like her older children playing in the new neighborhood because there is limited yard space and the neighboring children are "streetwise." She would like to move to a larger home in a nearby community, which would be closer to her parents who have been supportive both emotionally and financially.

Sandy was not employed when living with her husband, but her husband's income provided a higher standard of living than what she is currently living on. She receives public assistance and food stamps, in addition to minimal child support from both husbands.

Sandy finds that she has little time away from the children and tension tends to build when she feels trapped. Her twelve-year-old daughter often feels resentment because she can't easily entertain friends or have any privacy in their home. This tension results in frequent arguments between Sandy and her daughter.

Recently, Sandy contacted the local Big Brother/Big Sister program for the two older children. She hopes that they will benefit from companionship that she is unable to provide because of her time with the two younger children. She might also gain relief from the tension she feels.

Sandy continues to struggle with the changes in her standard of living, neighborhood, relationship with her children, and personal pressures. There is a possibility she and her husband with reconcile their marriage, but they are working out their differences while living in separate communities.

Conclusion

Contemporary society increasingly witnesses the transition to single parenthood because of separation or divorce as a normative stressor. Single parent families are at risk for crises and need to learn how to perceive and cope with stress in order to adjust and adapt to the changes that occur.

Educational and counseling settings can influence the attainment of adaptive mechanisms, especially appropriate decision-making skills and use of social networks. This learning process should begin during childhood and continue into adulthood, so that when faced with crises, individuals and families have a reservoir of resources from which to draw.

References

ANGELL, R. C. *The Family Encounters the Depression*. New York:Charles Scribner (1936).

BERMAN, W. H. and D. C. Turk. "Adaptation to Divorce: Problems and Coping Strategies," *Journal of Marriage and the Family*, 43:179–189 (1981).

BLOOM, B. L., S. J. Asher, and S. W. White. "Marital Disruption as a Stressor: A Review and Analysis," *Psychological Bulletin*, 85:867–894 (1978).

BOHANNON, P. "The Six Stations of Divorce," in *Divorce and After*, P. Bohannon, ed., Garden City, NY:Doubleday and Company (1970).

BOSS, P. "A Clarification of the Concept of Psychological Father Presence in Families Experiencing Ambiguity of Boundary," *Journal of Marriage and the Family*, 39:141–151 (1977).

BOSS, P. "Normative Family Stress: Family Boundary Changes Across the Life Span," *Family Relations*, 29:445–450 (1980).

BOULD, S. "Female-Headed Families: Personal Fate Control and the Provider Role," *Journal of Marriage and the Family*, 39:339–349 (1977).

BRANDWEIN, R. A. "After Divorce: A Focus on Single Parent Families," *Urban and Social Change Review*, 10:21–25 (1977).

BRANDWEIN, R. A., C. Brown, and E. Fox. "Women and Children Last: The Social Situation of Divorced Mothers and Their Families," *Journal of Marriage and the Family*, 36:498–514 (1974).

BRASSARD, J. "Ecology of Divorce: Case Study of Analysis of Personal and Social Networks and Mother–Child Interaction in Divorced and Married Families," paper presented at National Council on Family Relations Annual Meeting, Boston (1979).

BROWN, P. and R. Manela. "Changing Family Roles: Women and Divorce," *Journal of Divorce*, 1:315–328 (1978).

BUEHLER, C. and J. Hogan. "Managerial Behavior and Stress in Families Headed by Divorced Women," *Family Relations*, 29:525–532 (1980).

BURR, W. *Theory Construction and the Sociology of the Family*. New York:John Wiley & Sons (1973).

CAVAN, R. and K. Ranck. *The Family and the Depression*. Chicago:University of Chicago Press (1938).

CHIRIBOGA, D., A. Coho, J. A. Stein, and J. Roberts. "Divorce, Stress and Social Supports: A Study in Help-Seeking Behavior," *Journal of Divorce*, 2:121–135 (1979).

COLLETTA, N. "Support Systems after Divorce: Incidence and Impact," *Journal of Marriage and the Family,* 4:837–846 (1979).

COLLETTA, N. "Stressful Lives: The Situation of Divorced Mothers and Their Children," *Journal of Divorce,* 6:19–31 (1983).

EDDY, W. B., S. M. Paap, and D. M. Glad. "Solving Problems in Living: The Citizen's Viewpoint," *Mental Hygiene,* 54:64–72 (1970).

ESPENSHADE, T. "The Economic Consequences of Divorce," *Journal of Marriage and the Family,* 41:615–625 (1979).

FERRI, E. "Characteristics of Motherless Families," *British Journal of Social Work,* 3:91–100 (1973).

GASSER, R. and C. Taylor. "Role Adjustment of Single-Parent Fathers with Dependent Children," *The Family Coordinator,* 25:397–401 (1976).

GLASSER, P. and E. Navarre. "Structural Problems of the One-Parent Family," *Journal of Social Issues,* 214:98–109 (1965).

GOODE, W. *After Divorce,* New York:The Free Press (1956).

HETHERINGTON, E. M., M. Cox, and R. Cox. "Divorced Fathers," *The Family Coordinator,* 25:417–428 (1976).

HETHERINGTON, E. M., M. Cox, and R. Cox. "Stress and Coping in Divorce: A Focus on Women," in *Psychology and Transition*, J. Gullahorn, ed., New York:B. H. Winston & Sons (1978).

HILL, R. "Generic Features of Families Under Stress," *Social Casework,* 39:139–150 (1958).

HOGAN, J. M., C. Buehler, and B. Robinson. "Single Parenting: Transitioning Alone," in *Stress and the Family. I: Coping with Normative Transitions,* H. I. McCubbin and C. R. Figley, eds., New York:Brunner/Mazel (1983).

KAYAK, A. E. and J. A. Linney. "Stress, Coping, and Life Change in the Single-Parent Family," *American Journal of Community Psychology,* 11:207–220 (1983).

KEITH, P. M. and R. B. Schafer. "Correlates of Depression Among Single Parent, Employed Women," *Journal of Divorce,* 5:49–59 (1982).

KOOS, E. *Families in Trouble.* New York:King's Crown Press (1946).

LEVINGER, G. "A Social-Psychological Perspective on Marital Dissolution," *Journal of Social Issues,* 32:21–47 (1976).

McCUBBIN, H. I., P. Boss, L. R. Wilson, and G. R. Lester. "Developing Family Invulnerability to Stress: Coping Patterns and Strategies Wives Employ in Managing Family Separations," in *The Family in Change,* J. Trost, ed., Wasters, Sweden: International Library (1980).

McCUBBIN, H. I. and C. R. Figley, eds. *Stress and the Family. I: Coping with Normative Transitions.* New York:Brunner/Mazel (1983).

McCUBBIN, H. I. and J. M. Patterson. *Systematic Assessment of Family Stress, Resources and Coping: Tools for Research, Education and Clinical Intervention.* St. Paul, MN:Family Social Science (1981).

McCUBBIN, H. I. and J. M. Patterson. "Family Adaptation to Crisis," in *Family Stress, Coping, and Social Support,* H. McCubbin, E. Cauble, and J. Patterson, eds., Springfield, IL:Charles C. Thomas Publisher (1982).

McCUBBIN, H. I. and J. M. Patterson. "Family Transitions: Adaptation to Stress," in

Stress and the Family. I: Coping with Normative Transitions, H. I. McCubbin and C. R. Figley, eds., New York:Brunner/Mazel (1983a).

MCCUBBIN, H. I. and J. M. Patterson. "The Family Stress Process: A Double ABCX Model of Adjustment and Adaptation," in *Advances and Developments in Family Stress Theory and Research*, H. McCubbin, M. Sussman, and J. Patterson, eds., New York:Haworth Press (1983b).

MCLANAHAN, S. S., N. V. Wedemeyer, and T. Adelberg. "Network Structure, Social Support and Psychological Well-Being in the Single-Parent Family," *Journal of Marriage and the Family*, 43:601–612 (1981).

MENDES, H. A. "Single Fathers," *The Family Coordinator*, 25:439–444 (1976).

MILLER, A. A. "Reactions of Friends to Divorce," in *Divorce and After*, P. Bohannon, ed., Garden City, NY:Doubleday and Company (1970).

OLSON, D. H. and H. I. McCubbin. "The Circumplex Model of Marital and Family Systems. VI: Application to Family Stress and Crisis Intervention," in *Family Stress, Coping, and Social Support*, H. I. McCubbin, A. E. Cauble, and J. M. Patterson, eds., Springfield, IL:Charles C. Thomas (1982).

ORTHNER, D. K., T. Brown, and D. Ferguson. "Single-Parent Fatherhood: Emerging Lifestyle," *The Family Coordinator*, 25:429–437 (1976).

PAOLUCCI, B., O. Hall, and N. Axinn. *Family Decision Making: An Ecosystem Approach*. New York:John Wiley & Sons (1977).

PEARLIN, L. I. and C. Schooler. "The Structure of Coping," *Journal of Health and Social Behavior*, 19:2–21 (1978).

PETT, M. G. "Predictors of Satisfactory Social Adjustment of Divorced Single Parents," *Journal of Divorce*, 5:1–17 (1982).

PICHITINO, J. P. "Profile of the Single Father: A Thematic Integration of the Literature," *The Personnel and Guidance Journal*, 61:295–300 (1983).

ROSENBLATT, A. and J. E. Mayer. "Help Seeking for Family Problems: A Survey of Utilization and Satisfaction," *American Journal of Psychiatry*, 128:1136–1140 (1972).

SANTROCK, J. W. and R. A. Warshak. "Father Custody and Social Development in Boys and Girls," *Journal of Social Issues*, 35:112–125 (1979).

SCHLESINGER, B. "The One-Parent Family: An Overview," *The Family Life Coordinator*, 15:133–138 (1966).

SMITH, R. M. and C. W. Smith. "Child Rearing and Single-Parent Fathers," *Family Relations*, 30:411–417 (1981).

SPANIER, G. and R. Casto. "Adjustment to Separation and Divorce: Quantitative Analysis," in *Divorce and Separation*, G. Levinger and O. Moles, eds., New York:Basic Books (1979).

TAYLOR, L. "The Effects of a Non-Related Adult Friend on Children of Divorce," *Journal of Divorce*, 5:67–76 (1982).

TURNER, J. T., W. W. Kimbrough, and R. N. Traynhan. "A Survey of Community Perceptions of Critical Life Situations and Community Helping Sources as a Tool for Mental Health Development," *Journal of Community Psychology*, 5:225–230 (1977).

VICTOR, I. and W. A. Winkler. *Fathers and Custody*, New York:Hawthorne (1977).

WEDEMEYER, N. W. and J. M. Johnson. "Learning the Single-Parent Role: Overcoming Traditional Marital-Role Influences," *Journal of Divorce*, 6:41–53 (1982).

WEISS, R. S. *Marital Separation.* New York:Basic Books (1975).

WEISS, R. S. "The Emotional Impact of Marital Separation," *Journal of Social Issues,* 32:135–146 (1976).

WEISS, R. S. "The Impact of Marital Dissolution on Income and Consumption in Single-Parent Households," *Journal of Marriage and the Family,* 46:115–127 (1984).

YATES, M. *Coping: A Survival Manual for Women Alone.* Englewood Cliffs, NJ: Prentice-Hall (1976).

Single Parenting and Stress

GEORGIANNA M. CORNELIUS

Introduction

THE TERM "SINGLE parent" is subject to a variety of interpretations. Single parenting extends beyond the idea of one biological or adoptive parent. Single parenting can refer to extended families that may include grandparents, aunts, uncles, or other adults in the home. The single parent may be the adult who has chosen not to marry or the individual who selected adoption. There are a multitude of circumstances that involve single parenting. Although desertion and divorce are major causes of single parenthood, non-marriage, continued widowhood, or adoption are choices commonly selected by adults.

The reality is that a multitude of single adults are parenting alone. Single parents are beyond the stereotype myth of the low-income minority family. Single parents are well represented by many racial backgrounds and come from a wide range of socioeconomic classes. Single parents represent a diverse group of individuals which is rapidly increasing in all parts of the country, rural and urban.

The choice of single parenting involves a complex pattern of decision making, frequently done alone. The single parent must be aware of his/her own values as a distinct individual and as a member of a culture. They face the never-ending task of deciding which child-rearing methods to employ, what value system to live by, and what specific behaviors to model for their children. Parenting is a continuous, changing process of growth for individual parent and for the child. Just as parents within an intact family learn to become

parents, single parents must grow and learn the role and responsibilities of single parenting. This new role involves many more decisions and responsibilities since the single parent assumes the responsibility of primary decision maker and is the most single
important influence on the child.

The present chapter is organized into three major sections. First,
the complex role of the single parent is presented and described in
relation to identified tasks. The focus of this section will help the
reader better understand the multiple roles of the single parent.

The second section addresses the sources of stress in the single
parent. These include: (1) economic issues, (2) specific needs of the
child, (3) time, (4) conflicts over child rearing, and (5) employment
issues. The third section examines research studies that have been
conducted to investigate parental stress and young children.

The Complex Role of the Single Parent

The single parent role may be one of the most difficult and complex
roles in our society. Single parenting is further complicated by the
fact that most adults are not prepared to assume the responsibilities
of the role (LeMasters and DeFrain, 1983; Rossi, 1969). For example,
a greater number of young teenagers are becoming pregnant and
choosing to raise their offspring. Other reasons lie in the lack of
available parenting education and inadequate modelling of positive
parental behaviors.

Pasley and Gecas (1982) examined the stresses and satisfactions of
the parental role. They suggested that the parental role was poorly
defined, ambiguous, and not adequately delimited. This confusing,
over-demanding role of parenting pressed the adult into a more restrictive, authoritarian style of parenting (Weiss, 1980; Hetherington, Cox, and Cox, 1982). Both men and women feel a role strain
when they are individually responsible for the economic and the
family decisions. This role of parenting becomes even more complex
when one parent must assume the major tasks of a family. For example, the one parent is responsible to rear the children, maintain a
warm, nurturing environment, and provide opportunities for each
family member to develop competence and individuality. Obviously,
parenting goes beyond the concepts of guiding and protecting the
children.

Child rearing requires time, energy, and good health. For example,
it takes time to meet the primary needs of the child, particularly if
the child is under the age of five years. The task of parenting
becomes even more demanding if the child has a physical or emo-

tional handicap. On the other hand, what about the parent who has an individual handicap or is physically restricted in some way?

Fashioning a warm, nurturing environment that meets the needs of family members is an equally important task of the parent. When finances and time are limited, it is difficult for most individuals to be responsive and positive. The important issue to recognize is that single parents are not superhuman, but frequently society expects them to be. *true!*

Certainly, quality time in sharing activities, ideas, and feelings is critical in helping the child define his individuality. Time with the child for the single parent frequently is hard to maintain.

Employment and personal issues may consume a great deal of parent–child time. However, in strengthening the family and building and maintaining positive interaction, an investment of shared time is critical. *family tasks*

Saul Brown (1978) described four major tasks of a family: (1) establishing basic commitments to family members, (2) providing warmth and nurturance for all members, (3) providing opportunities and encouraging the development of individuality, and (4) facilitating ego mastery and competence. When these basic four tasks are applied and related to the needs and abilities of one adult, the challenge of parenting becomes critical. More specifically, the parent is responsible for fostering all facets of the child's growth. It is the task of the parent to select and implement appropriate strategies to reach these goals.

The Multiple Tasks of the Single Parent

Fortunately, parenting is a learned skill (Brooks, 1986). Frequently, as a single parent the adult assumes multiple responsibilities. For example, the parent is now the head of the household and responsible for building and maintaining economic stability. Rent, utilities, food, and recreation are all part of that ongoing process of financing a home and family. Expenses involve medical, school, day care, and a variety of needs. First, single parents need to identify ① realistic expectations within their new role as the primary caregiver of their child. These expectations must be realistic and acceptable to the individual's value system. What type of employment is available? What kind of job am I qualified and interested in? How many hours do I want to work and is it close to my child's school? Choices of housing are similar concerns. Should I move into another area that is more economically reasonable? Do I want to live in the suburbs or in the city? Should I move in with my sister in the country home? In turn, the parents must have *realistic* expectations of their children. Are the expectations that I have for my child reasonable ones?

For example, should my children share in the responsibility of household chores? Do I expect too much of Susan, in helping out around the house? Frequently, single parents have been found to be overprotective in the areas of fostering more independent behaviors because of guilt from the divorce. Research has shown that mothers and fathers overcompensate for the missing parent and attempt to do and provide everything for the child.

This overcompensation is not a healthy solution to very important needs of any of the family members. On a realistic level, one parent cannot successfully meet all the child's needs, nor can the child meet the parent's expectations. The need for friendships, support groups, and significant other adults is vital for the single parent family's well-being.

Modelling

Certainly, the task of the single parent is not an easy one. It involves the continuous task of modelling appropriate behaviors so that the child can be guided by a positive influence. This modelling of appropriate behaviors does not begin when the child becomes a preschooler, nor does it end when the child enters elementary school. Personal example has consistently been shown to be critical in children's development.

It is this process of parenting that allows reflection and opportunities for change and improvement. For example, for the parent who desires to have a child adopt better eating habits, direct demonstration and modelling of such healthy habits is most effective. Similarly, for parents who strive to encourage reading in their children, research has repeatedly shown that modelling of such behavior has the most impact. Parents who read usually have children who read (Holdaway, 1979).

Honesty and Trust

Honesty and trust in the parent–child relationship is another critical task of the parent. Effective parenting places tremendous demands on the single parent. The single parent must be able to communicate needs clearly, which may be a difficult task to do if it elicits a guilty feeling of being an inadequate or an unresponsive parent. Trust is an issue for single parents because they must have confidence in their parenting ability and be able to cope with the demands of friends, family, work, and society in general. Alone, they must face problems, seek solutions, and continue to model a positive parenting role. Again, the dictates of being a single parent does not mean the parent should try to assume a "Super parent" role. Facing problems involves the cognitive recognition of the reality situation. This does not imply acceptance, but rather an active awareness that one is a single parent with responsibilities. Seeking solutions means an active search of support, alternatives to problems, and creative solutions. This may involve joining a support group, participating in a baby-sitting cooperative, and planning and implementing a manageable budget.

Communication

Another equally important task and responsibility of the single parent is communication. The complex task of spending the time and attention with your child to express concern, love, and interest is needed. This is a very difficult area of concern for single parents, particularly if one is employed. Time may be extremely limited for the single parent, and the quality of time with the child becomes an issue. This communication between the parent and child is vital for a mutual understanding and appreciation of family members. Shared viewpoints, problem solving, and affection are just a few positive benefits of open, clear communication between parent and child.

Some important guidelines may include:

(1) Schedule a realistic amount of time for primary tasks such as meals, getting ready for school, and related activities.
(2) Schedule a special time each day (even for ten minutes) to share intimate concerns and ideas. Make this time a period of genuine listening and sharing.
(3) Make an active effort to communicate to family members that they are in fact special and unique. Lunch box notes, a note on the door, surprise messages inside socks, or even a telephone call open the door for more positive communication.
(4) Actively make changes in household based on shared ideas and thoughts.
(5) Select an activity that you and your child may enjoy and spend weekly time doing it.

Respect

Respect for the child and respect for oneself are vital tasks of the single parent. This involves recognizing and acknowledging the needs of the child as well as your own. For a healthy relationship, in-

interaction and consideration are necessary ingredients. The task of respect is an all-important one to model in the home. Because the parent and child are unique individuals, it is important to recognize and appreciate these differences.

Respect for the child involves a great deal. Does the home environment reflect the needs of the child? Is there adequate space for the child to engage in a variety of activities? Is the home designed for an adult in that all furniture and furnishings accommodate only an adult?

Respect can be demonstrated by providing low shelves for toys, furniture that is child size, and adequate space for large and small motor activities. Usually, the child's art work and projects can be displayed as wall hangings or centerpieces for the table.

On a more cognitive level, the child can be given leadership responsibilities such as creating the dinner menu, setting the table, or selecting the cereal for breakfast. Encouraging and fostering more mature independent behaviors from the young child is best handled through acceptance and respect.

The Sources of Stress for the Single Parent

The sources of stress experienced by mothers are numerous. For example, a father's absence from the household is often examined as the major cause of stress (Lamb, 1982; Brandwein, 1974; Lewis and Weinraub, 1976; Weinraub, 1978). Economic stress is frequently cited as a major stress issue. Others (Weiss, 1984; Espenshade, 1979; Cocoran, 1979) explored economic problems as a major contributor to the mother's stress. Economic difficulties, father absence, and increased parenting responsibilities contribute to the stress experienced as a single parent. A great deal of research has examined parental stress and how it affects the young child. While a considerable amount of research has examined the stress of parenting, few studies have explored the number of stressors and the interaction of those factors.

Specific Needs of the Child

A second stressor suggested was the actual presence of children. A child who is having emotional or physical difficulties in development within the family may create stress in the parent (Abidin, 1984). Similarly, tremendous stress may result when a parent does not have the knowledge or understanding of young children's development to comprehend fully what is happening in the home. For example, for a parent who does not understand the assertive verbal language of the growing and developing toddler, this results in conflict. This very natural behavior may be viewed in a very negative manner and responded to with very angry adult language or inappropriate physical reactions. Stress may be the result of having two or more children who are extremely close in chronological age. The responsibility of caring for more than one child under the age of four may be too great a responsibility for the parent. The nurturing and caring of one child becomes an overwhelming burden when the parent's time is completely consumed in primary tasks of feeding, diapering, and caring for children.

The developmental needs of the preschooler are distinctly different from that of the toddler, the adolescent, or the changing teenager. The physical and cognitive competency of the toddler dictates very specific interactions and responses from the adult when compared to other age levels.

Even when children are developmentally close in age, the uniqueness of children's personalities, learning styles, and temperaments makes parenting a challenge. What seemed an effective style with one child may fail miserably with the second one.

Needs of the Parent

Limited time for solitude, adult activities, and quiet time for the couple were designated as critical issues. Frequently, a new birth of a child changes a couple's schedule and, more specifically a parent's leisure time. Conflict and readjustment are common particularly if the parent or couple have been independent without children for a long time. Also, if the child requires a great deal of attention because of emotional or physical needs, the parent may experience stress and severely limited amounts of time for other activities.

The needs of the parent are extremely important. Frequently, parents feel the needs of the child must be satisfied first. However, research (Brown, 1978) has consistently shown that parents critically need to reflect on their individuality and schedule meaningful time for themselves. This may involve a variety of sports, recreational activities, or even a peaceful walk each evening. The need for "parent time" is so important for one's own growth and life interests. Not only is the parent satisfying a personal need for individual growth, but also modelling an active interest in life to their children.

The needs of the parent extend beyond simple private time. Physical and emotional growth is sometimes ignored or tolerated and replaced by intense focusing upon the growth and development of children. Physical activities for social enjoyment and health are valuable in helping the active parent stay active and healthy (LeMasters and DeFrain, 1983). Emotionally, the single parent needs to carve out a path of social, meaningful activities. This may range from an occasional lunch with a friend to a movie with a group of friends. Parent associations like Parents without Partners are excellent organizations that involve parents in enjoyable activities. Obviously, a healthy and happy adult is more likely to parent in a more positive manner.

Conflicts over Child Rearing

Disputes between spouses over child-rearing issues may be another source of stress. Conflicts and disagreements over how to discipline the child are frequently cited topics. Severe stress was reported when children required the most care during infancy and the preschool years. This period of time was described as one of constant primary care and monitoring. Parents felt that their time was consumed by the child's needs. When there is a lack of consensus regarding acceptable behaviors, discipline, and bedtime issues, conflict occurs within the marriage.

Similarly, the single parent faces internal conflict as a solitary decision maker. What is the best time for children to go to bed? Does my child always have to eat what he takes at dinner time? Am I too rigid or too flexible with certain behaviors? The single parent's decisions may come into conflict with peers or other family members as to what constitutes appropriate parenting. For example, in an extended family where the single parent has moved back home, disagreements may occur. What worked for the single parent's mother may be completely inappropriate. This conflict of child-rearing values creates a great deal of stress for the parent assuming sole responsibility in caring for the child.

Employment

Another important stressor was attributed to the parent–child relationship, particularly when the parent was employed (Brooks, 1985; Weiss, 1984). Employment for the parent involves adjustment and readjustment of the family schedule. The parent–child relationship changes due to changes in employment. This is particularly true if the child previously stayed home with one of the parents. The parent must now investigate daycare possibilities, and secure care for her child while she is at work. The parent must invest additional time to examine issues of quality care, location and accessibility of the day care center, and the affordability of the care. For elementary school children, this new employment status of the parent poses additional outside care for time after school. Issues of transportation to and from the caregiver are also readjustments for the parent and child.

A new job poses changes in the mealtime schedule of the home and how time is spent outside of the work situation. An employment commitment changes the amount of time a parent and child have for leisure activities. If the parent assumes the responsibilities of an extremely demanding position, this in turn creates stress for the parent and the child. Similarly, if the parent assumes a position which has rigid work hours or extended shifts, the demands made of the parent may be too great and the situation too severe for the child.

This transitional phase of the mother entering or re-entering the work force may create stress and turmoil in the home until a more stable, predictable schedule is worked out. Frequently, women have had little psychological, educational, or occupational preparation. When men separate and are divorced, they are more adequately prepared economically to assume the new role. For women who have been full-time mothers, they are frequently too limited in their training, skills, and educational background to make the transition a smooth one. For many single women, they must accept jobs at lower salaries than men and work at jobs that offer little satisfaction or opportunity for advancement.

Research Studies on Parental Stress

Pasley and Gecas (1982) interviewed 136 families and presented a questionnaire of closed- and open-ended questions focusing on perceptions of parenthood. Results showed that pre-adolescent and post-adolescent periods were the most difficult child-rearing years. A second result was that those parents who chose the preschool years as the most difficult saw themselves as responsible for the difficulty. Specifically, parents reported lack of patience and skills as reasons for the difficulty. Third, more mothers reported the burdensome nature of caring for young children than did fathers.

In a recent study by Cornelius (1986), forty parents were interviewed regarding their stress and attitudes about children's play. All subjects were parents of preschool children ranging from four to five-

and-one-half years of age. Half the sample came from intact families, and the other half were single parents. There was no significant difference in the stress reported by the two groups of parents. However, thirty-eight of the forty parents reported moderate to high levels of stress. Upon closer examination of the data, stress was attributed to parenting skills rather than individual problems with the child. This seems to be consistent with the results of Pasley and Gecas (1982) in that parents of preschool children perceived these years as very demanding ones which require a great deal of patience and time.

In an earlier study, Colletta (1983) examined how family stress varies with family structure (one or two parents) and income level. The sample involved seventy-two divorced and married women at two income levels. Of the total sample, forty-eight were divorced women and twenty-four were married women. An open-ended interview approach was used to investigate stress and child-rearing practices. Ten stress variables were identified. These were:

(a) Neighborhood
(b) Care arrangements
(c) Living arrangements
(d) Employment
(e) Housework and errands
(f) Health
(g) Financial
(h) Community service
(i) Child care information
(j) Child rearing

There were nine child-rearing variables utilized. Results showed that when families differed only in family structure there were significant differences only in stresses associated with caring for children, maintaining a household, financial resources for family, and neighborhood concerns. When families with the same income were compared, the two groups were found to differ only in overall stress, financial stress, child-rearing stress, stress associated with community services, employment, and living arrangement stress.

The researchers (Colletta, 1983) concluded that low-income divorced mothers faced multiple stresses because of father absence and low income. The low-income mothers focused on poverty and poverty related issues such as inadequate living arrangements, unsatisfactory jobs, and the need for public assistance. While most of the stress was related to financial stress, the investigators concluded that the maternal role without assistance from the father was a critical issue. This finding has serious implications in relation to the increasing evidence of divorced couples failing to psychologically or financially support one another following a divorce or separation. Many women who assume full custody and care of the children following divorce, when compared to men, report fewer opportunities for social and sexual relationships because of economic and time constraints (Brooks, 1985).

Generally, families of divorce encountered many more stresses and difficulties in coping which were associated with personal and social adjustments of family members than the nondivorced families. Mother-headed households were exposed to excessive stresses with minimal support systems. Most women are not adequately prepared to assume complete responsibility for supporting the family, taking care of the household, and raising the children. Similarly, men are ill-prepared to handle the multiple facets of family life. This is particularly true if the father is only familiar with the roles of breadwinner and part-time father.

In an earlier study by Hetherington et al. (1976) similar results were found. For example, female heads of families felt severe stress in running a household without support. Heatherington et al. studied the impact of divorce on families and the development of children after two years had passed. A second goal related to the stressors, support systems, family functioning, and developmental status of children in divorced and nondivorced families. The sample consisted of seventy-two parents and children.

Measures used in the study included interviews, structured diaries, observations of parent–child interactions, behavior checklists of child behavior, parent rating of the child's behavior, and a battery of personality scales on the parents. Observations of the children were conducted in nursery schools and homes. Parents and children were administered these measures two months, one year, and two years following divorce. In addition, a six-year follow-up study was conducted.

Data analysis involved a repeated measures multivariate analysis of variance which included test session, sex of child, sex of parent, and family composition (divorced versus nondivorced). Results showed many differences between the intact and divorced families.

In family functioning, parent–child relations improved but were still strained even after two years following the divorce. Divorced parents made fewer maturity demands of their children, communicated less effectively, were less affectionate, disciplined inconsistently, and lacked control with their children more than nondivorced parents.

Weinraub and Wolf (1983) investigated the social networks, coping abilities, life stresses, and mother–child interaction with twenty-eight mother–child pairs. This sample included fourteen single mothers and their preschool children and fourteen matched married women and their children. Procedurally, a questionnaire was used to measure the mother's social network, coping abilities, and stress. Observation of the mother and child yielded information about maternal control, demands, nurturance, communication, and child compliance. Analysis of the data involved matched t-tests between single and two parent families in stress, social supports, coping, and parent–child interactions. Pearson product correlations were obtained between these variables.

Results of the investigation revealed that single parents face more stressful life changes than do their married counterparts, have fewer coping abilities and few support systems. The quality of the mother–child interaction was significantly different for the two family structures since stress tended to be related to less positive mother–child interactions. In both family structures stressful events were associated with reduced maternal nurturance and less positive communication. However, single parent families displayed greater stress than dual parent families. Social contacts for single parents were related to less parental nurturances, but for married parents the frequency of contacts was not related.

Research on the stress of single and dual parent families suggests several important conclusions. First, single parents generally face a substantially greater number of stressors than do dual parent households (Pasley and Gecas, 1984; Weiss, 1984; Colletta, 1983). Compared to married individuals, the single parent operates multiple functions, spends more time working and less time with his/her children, and has fewer support systems and social contacts.

Consequently, the child from a single parent home spends a greater number of hours in child care, has limited parent access, less consistent time with the parent, and experiences more frequent changes involving housing and schedules than does a child from a dual parent family (Weinraub and Wolf, 1983; Wallerstein, 1980; Lamb, 1982; Hetherington, Cox, and Cox, 1982). Finally, the parent–child interaction between these two family structures is substantially different. For example, in the single parent household there is less positive verbal communication, lower maturity expectations, and a greater number of restrictions (Levy-Shiff, 1982; Colletta, 1983).

Summary

In summary, within the family, the number of adults in the home and stress were found to be related to less positive mother–child interactions, fewer resources, and the single parent household, where resources of space, time, energy, and materials are limited. For women, these stressors are more pronounced because they earn substantially less, average fewer years of education, and are less prepared to earn a living than males (Brooks, 1984; Schorr, 1979). There exists no easy solutions or quickly prescribed antidotes for the complex responsibility of parenting. What does exist for the increasing number of adults who are becoming single parents are workable solutions that require time and commitment.

Certainly, in the sense of resolving problems or issues in our lives, one must identify optimistic yet realistic solutions. The complex problems and issues that surround single parenting are numerous. The emotional demands of parenting alone are endless. The financial issues are equally overwhelming. Fortunately, a single parent can cope and deal with these difficulties in a constructive problem-solving manner. Through consistent modelling, open communication, and serious commitment to resolving those issues, the single parent can create and achieve a rewarding life. This continuous process (Brooks, 1985; Watson and Fischer, 1986) requires careful examination of the needs and changes within the family. A large part of this examination requires the single parent to recognize his/her own needs, the child's needs, and the importance of supportive friends. Resourcefulness, flexibility, and reflection are integral parts of this growth in the single parent.

References

ABIDIN, R. R. *Parenting Stress Index-Manual.* Charlottesville, VA:Pediatric Psychology Press (1983).

BLOOM, B. *Stability and Change Characteristics.* New York:Wiley (1961).

BRANDWEIN, R. A., C. A. Brown, and E. M. Fox. "Women and Children Last: The Social Situation of Divorced Mothers and Their Families," *Journal of Marriage and the Family,* 36:498–514 (1974).

BROOKS, J. B. *The Process of Parenting.* Mayfield Publishing Co. (1985).

BROWN, S. "Functions, Tasks and Stresses of Parenting Implications or Guidance," in *Helping Parents Help Their Children,* L. Eugene Arnold, ed., New York:Bruner/Mazel, pp. 22–35 (1978).

COCORAN, M. E. "The Economic Consequences of Marital Dissolution for Women in the Middle Years," *Sex Roles,* 5:343–353 (1979).

COLLETTA, N. "Stressful Lives: The Situation of Divorced Mothers and Their Children," *Journal of Divorce,* 6(3):19–31 (1983).

ESPENSHADE, T. J. "The Economic Consequences of Divorce," *Journal of Marriage and the Family,* 41:615–624 (1979).

HETHERINGTON, E., M. Cox, and R. Cox. "Effects of Divorce on Parents and Children," in *Nontraditional Families: Parenting and Child Development,* M. E. Lamb, ed., Lawrence Erlbaum Associates, Inc. (1982).

HOLDAWAY, D. *The Foundations of Literacy.* NH: Heineman Educational Books, Inc. (**1979**).

LAMB, M. E. *Nontraditional Families: Parenting and Child Development.* Lawrence Erlbaum Associates, Inc. (1982).

LEMASTERS, M. M. and J. DeFrain. *Parenting in Contemporary America* (4th ed.). Homewood, IL:Dorsey Press (1983).

LEWIS, M. and M. Weinraub. "The Fathers' Role in the Child's Social Network," in *The Role of the Father in Child Development,* M. Lamb, ed. (1976).

PASLEY, K. and V. Gecas. "Stresses and Satisfaction of the Parental Role," *Personnel & Guidance Journal,* 62(7):400–404 (1984).

ROSSI, S. "Transition to Parenthood," *Journal of Marriage and the Family,* 30:26–39 (1969).

SCHORR, A. and P. Moen. "The Single Parent and Public Policy," *Social Policy,* 9(5):15–21 (1979).

WALLERSTEIN, J. "Children of Divorce: Stress and Developmental Tasks," in *Stress, Coping and Development in Children.* McGraw-Hill Book Co. (1983).

WALLERSTEIN, J. and J. B. Kelly. "Effects of Divorce on the Father–Child Relationship," *American Journal of Psychiatry,* 137:1534–1539 (1978).

4.

CHAPTER 5

Dynamics of the Parent–Child Relationship in Single Parent Families

ONCE A FAMILY weathers the questioning and doubt of the emotional separation that precedes divorce, once they survive the struggle and compromise of the legal separation, the outcome is a single parent family or two single parent families in fortunate circumstances. In some families it is the death of a spouse that produces a single parent family. The once-married adults in these single parent families have two distinct phenomena to address in their relationships with their children: the creation of single parent status and the reality of life in a single parent household. Having once had an intact, dual parent family, once-married adults must face the adjustments required by the newly arisen single parent status.

Two other sets of single parent families deal only with the latter issue since there was no marriage relationship from the start. Unwed mothers must raise their children without the formal cooperation of the biological father. It is the traditional husband–wife, mother–child, and father-child triad of relationships that is absent in these families, regardless of the support available from parents or others. With the changes in state adoption laws, some adoptive parents are also single by choice, formalizing a relationship to a child but not to a mate. The never-married adults in these single parent families may be questioned about their choice to raise children without a spouse, but in reality they deal with the absence of a spousal relationship and a second parent–child relationship, not with the disruption of them.

It is also the case that some military families undergo periods when they function both like and unlike single parent families. When military personnel are deployed from base, the families left behind must deal with the realities of life in a sole parent household as well as help sustain a viable relationship between the absent parent and his or her children. It is the consecutive independence and interdependence within these families that creates many special needs. Adults and children alike must adapt to the changing needs to be at times capable of self-reliance and independent problem solving while at other times capable of intimacy and compromise. There are, of course, other government and business families who experience similar patterns of having one spouse successively in town and out of town. Seasonal workers, field engineers, territorial sales staff, and international corporate representatives come to mind as examples of adults whose families undergo successive sole parenting.

In this chapter we will examine the issues specific to the parent–child relationship in single parent families. Whether death, divorce, unwed status, adoptive status, or military status produces the single parent family, certain issues arise that are not pertinent to parent–child interactions in intact families. All families must rear and socialize their children, but single parent families must do so without the services of a second contributing adult. In addition, single parents who were once married must contend with the changes in the child's relationship to the absent spouse. Considering the varied nature of single parent status, then, the information presented here will apply to some types more than others. The majority of the coverage will pertain to families of divorce because of the range of issues they face. Direct application to the other types of families mentioned can be made wherever applicable.

Comprehensive coverage of the dynamics of parent–child relationships in single parent families across the life span would generate several manuscripts, each relating to some special circumstance of the adult's life coinciding with the age status of the child or children. In this chapter the intent is to provide an overview of the unique dynamics that arise between parents and children in single parent households during childhood and early adolescence. Our focus is on the search for well-being by families in which one adult is responsible for a child or children. We will examine the events likely to occur and will consider ways in which families might best avoid the pitfalls to successful relationships.

The Search for Well-Being

The phenomenon of divorce is typically viewed as a crisis event (Belsky, Lerner, and Spanier, 1984). Just a decade ago, knowing that a child came from a "broken home" gave rise to feelings of pity and concern and to predictions of distress and disturbance, even delinquency. It is interesting to note that divorce has less of a sociological connotation in contemporary prose, and mention of a "broken home" is exceedingly rare in this era of rising divorce rates. Whether or not the precipitating factors to divorce in a family are disruptive in nature, the very divorce itself gives rise to multiple changes for all family members. For the spouse who leaves, the one who is left, or the partners who choose to let go, there is a search for a return to well-being. Children benefit if the adults who care for them address questions of well-being as well as questions of care and protection. Children's questions often communicate the need to know not just who or what will happen but also whether or not they will be okay through it all.

Some of the questions arise from the new family lifestyle; others indicate unfinished business regarding the dissolution of the family unit. The legal decree is no guarantee that children, or even adults, have sorted through all the concerns generated by the divorce. In the midst of change, and often turmoil, realistic appraisal and caring responses to questions and fears help restore a sense of well-being in the lives of parents and children. It is a fine line to tread between secrecy and confusion on the one hand and melodrama and loyalty ploys on the other. Too little information about the adult realities that led to the divorce decision leaves children at the mercy of their own fears and fantasies in attempting to understand what has happened. Too much information is a great burden to children, with specific details proving to be more seductive and provocative or more alarming and anxiety-provoking than children can handle. Adults who are forthright yet cautious in meeting children's concerns reap dividends in the form of their children's healthy functioning.

Questions of Time, Place, and Causality

Children who are new to a situation of divorce have many thoughts and feelings about what is happening. They raise questions about time, place, and causality concerning divorce, that is questions of when, where, and why they must face changes in their lives. According to the age and reasoning ability of the child, the questions are likely to differ. It is the cognitive developmental view of children's thought that gives us clues to the forms these questions are likely to take (Piaget, 1954, 1955, 1959, 1960, 1970; Piaget and Inhelder, 1967). Contemporary theorists recognize that children exhibit more sophisticated reasoning in questions derived from their own experiences rather than in response to questions posed by adults (Gelman, 1972; Carlson, 1976; Greenfield, 1976). Viewing the divorce decision as an adult phenomenon, we would expect children to demonstrate the more traditional stage-progression in reasoning, though this is still a matter of conjecture open for verification.

Preschool Years

In early childhood, children are most concerned with immediate experiences of here and now. They judge events on the basis of how things appear. Their questions might be of the sort:

Time: "*When* will I see my daddy? I miss him now."
            "But it's *time* for a bath and I want Mommy to give me a bath, not you."

Place: "This is our *house*. I want to stay in my own room."
            "My *bed* is not in that apartment; it's here in our house."

Causality: "*Why* did Mommy go away? I want her here to hug and kiss me."
            "*Why* can't my daddy go to Grandma's house with us?"

The best response is a calm and matter-of-fact reply. Parents assist children and help them improve their own coping skills when they define and clarify the nature of the child's post-divorce life-to-be. In all the examples that follow, the exact words are not as important as the intent of the message. One set of possible replies appears here to demonstrate the impact of forthright and developmentally suitable responses by parents. To the respective child questions reported above, parents might reply:

Time: "Mommy can give you a bath tomorrow night. Tonight it's my turn."

Place: "Now you have two houses. In each one we'll make a space that belongs only to you."

Causality: "Daddy will visit at his mother's house and I will visit at my mother's house. You are welcome to visit at both houses."

Parents who recognize that children's comments involve both *thinking and feeling* will be best prepared to help their children develop the ability to cope with this unexpected occurrence, as well as those that might arise in the future. "I know you miss your daddy. Sometimes you feel so sad you want to cry. But your daddy will come to see you as soon as he is able."

Early School Years

With the advance to childhood, the questions take on features of social comparison and a search for underlying intentions. Children's concerns regarding time, place, and causality might be reflected in statements like:

Time:	"*When* it's my birthday, can I spend it with you and Mommy together?"
	"But I can't go to Daddy's *then!* I'll miss the school play!"
Place	"I don't like it at Daddy's *house.* My friends can't ride their bikes that far."
	"Don't make me share a *room* with Katie! I liked it when I had my room to myself."
Causality:	"*Why* did you and Mommy have to get divorced? Kevin's parents aren't divorced."
	"*If* you had tried harder, I bet you and Dad wouldn't argue so much."

Responses to questions at this level require a greater examination of the human condition without burdening the child with the specifics of the disintegration of the marriage relationship. Parents might attempt to reassure the child that each person, child or adult, retains general dignity and integrity despite the estimates resulting from social comparison and judgment. Possible parental responses include:

Time:	"Every parent would like to be with their child on his or her birthday. Sometimes that's not possible. In their heart, that's where they wish to be."
Place:	"You and your friends can work on making plans that are flexible enough for all of you. Every child spends some time with family and some time with friends. They're just not all free at the same time."
Causality:	"Every parent tries to make the very best decision they can about a family for their children. In some families, like ours, that means the parents make the difficult decision not to stay together."

When the child of elementary school age applies the rule of social comparison to pit parents against each other, both parents must join in refusing to escalate the competition. "I know your mom allows two snacks, but in my house we have only one snack. It's just two different ways. When you're with me you get one snack, when you're with your mom you get two."

Early Adolescence

Along with physical changes in adolescence come changes in social and cognitive skills as well. The advance to hypothetical thinking brings greater skills of analysis which adolescents apply to existing problems. At the same time, though, these new modes of thought help generate multiple possible scenarios that are more or less likely to occur, but still distressing to contemplate. Adolescents have the ability to pose the following questions:

Time: "*When* did you and Dad stop loving each other? If the two of you could stop loving each other, you might stop loving me next."

"Maybe it's not possible for any two people to stay together for a *life*time. I'm never going to get married."

Place: "I don't want to choose between your house and Mom's *house*. I'm old enough to take care of myself."

"There's no *place* for me in Dad's house. His wife won't even let me put my things out. She'll soon convince Dad not to waste his time on me."

Causality: "I'll never understand *why* two people would ever want to get married in the first place. All they do is hurt each other in the end. I think it's smarter to just live together and move out when the time comes."

"Now that I know *why* divorce is considered to be so painful, I will never marry anyone who believes in divorce. I will never put my kids through what I've been through."

The challenges of such questions at this age spring from many emotional chords: loss of respect for parents who appear to have failed, refusal to accept the new relationships each parent nurtures, and fear of one's own inability to establish intimate relations with one's own peers. Responses must help differentiate parent from off-spring, must convey the role of the unexpected in the unfolding of relationships, and must acknowledge the existence of "personal fables" in the lives of adolescents—the feeling that they alone are capable of all good (Elkind and Bowen, 1979). Parents assist adolescents in the construction of an understanding of human nature when they provide insights into the human condition that are respectful of human limitations yet optimistic regarding human intentions. Parents are likely to respond in the following ways:

Time: "Men and women choose their mates for marriage. But their children are their own flesh and blood. That blood relationship never ends."

Place: "You are old enough to begin to carve out your own niche in your dad's home and in mine. But you still need the care and protection we will continue to provide until you are on your own."

Causality: "Two people can't stop growing just because they marry. Sometimes they grow in ways that cannot be integrated into a family. It's not that love isn't big enough to embrace the growth. It's that love understands when to let go, knowing that two people cannot compromise their individual values in order to stay together."

There are people yet today who express great sorrow for children who must endure the disruption of divorce, implying that one would surely wish to spare children the hurt if only they could. And surely, if one could choose, one would always choose comfort over hardship. But I would like to offer a ray of hope in the midst of this gloom. At least on a societal level, perhaps this experience and training in the understanding of adult relations will help prepare today's adolescents to make life choices from a broader base of understanding. In exposing cherished myths about love and marriage, we operate instead from a stronger sense of the realities of human existence. Perhaps today's adolescents will be tomorrow's spouses capable of constructing marriages that withstand differences, distance, and adversity by relying on realistic expectations.

Broad Spectrum of Feelings

Children of all ages experience a range of feelings regarding life in a single parent family. Guilt, anger, depression, and fear are often exhibited through both verbal and non-verbal means. The youngest children worry that it was their misbehavior that forced one parent to leave. School-age children feel that they were the cause of their parents' arguments which resulted in diminishing the love that once existed. And adolescents entertain the possibility that they were unwanted children from accidental pregnancies who only contributed a source of unhappiness to their parents as they attempted to build a family from the ruins of their young lives.

A parent helps children resolve these emotional dilemmas just as they would with any other emotional experience such as the rejection felt in not receiving an expected invitation to a classmate's birthday party. First, they assist the child in labeling the emotions as accurately as possible. "Yes, you are feeling angry, sad, lonely, afraid, confused." They give information that aids in distinguishing between feelings. "You get angry when your friends talk about activities with their dads because it hurts you to know that your dad is so far away." And they help the child identify a plan of action resulting from the feelings. "You can take pictures of your science fair display to send to your mom. You know she will be proud of your work." The important message to convey is that real feelings are a part of real people. All of us will experience moments of despair and moments of exhilaration. Children are more likely to match action to emotion than adults are, consequently, there is a greater likelihood that children will be immobilized by strong emotion. Pursuing action despite emotion is a learned skill. As in all skill development, children are in the process of learning this skill and will be more or less successful depending on the situation. Parents can assist children by recommending diversions in situations of low intensity emotions like disappointment, only gradually building toward action in the face of strong emotion like feeling unloved.

The challenge for the single parent is to respond appropriately to children's concerns while in the midst of one's own emotional dramas. On any given day, a parent might be preoccupied with self-doubts, concerned with financial security, or distressed about his or her ability to rear children alone. Meanwhile, children raise concerns about school, about friends, about the family, about growing up. And a parent attempts to set aside his or her own concerns in order to be emotionally available to the child whenever possible. Not every encounter will result in a successful discussion. The important point to remember is that a major portion of children's concerns need to be addressed, and a parent serves as a model of emotional adaptability. Whatever time a parent invests in assisting a child to air feelings will be repaid in progress toward emotional maturity.

A child left to resolve emotional distress alone often distorts and magnifies selected features of an event until an irrational outcome results. A child might, for example, reason that it is angry words that make someone leave. If he or she then vows never to utter an angry word, great effort is expended to guard against a natural human response, and the value of anger as a signal for the need to seek clarification is lost. It is likely, moreover, that the child will react to being the target of angry words by anticipating the expected outcome that someone will leave. Then the fear gets expressed in any manner of distress or disturbance.

Irrational fears influence a child's thoughts and behaviors, producing actions that are out of the ordinary. One such fear is the fear of abandonment (Mahler, Pine, and Bergman, 1975). A child who lives with two parents has someone else to rely on whenever one parent is unavailable. But a child who lives with one parent has no recourse if that parent is physically or psychologically unavailable. If the fear of abandonment is intense enough, a child might resort to exaggerated behaviors in an attempt to retain the security of parental regard. Trailing the parent while in the house, watching out windows for the parent's return, nightmare images of injury to the parent, and rejecting the parent before first being rejected are indications that assurances need to be given with regard to the parent's continuing care for children and provisions for emergency situations. Discussing with children the realities of guardians to care for them if something happened to the parent is actually more reassuring than it is frightening to a child who fears abandonment. A parent need only take the child's lead, reading the signals of the child's behavior to raise the issue of the underlying feelings.

A second irrational fear is the fear of being unlovable. "If my own dad/mom couldn't find it in their heart to stay and love me," a child reasons, "how could anyone else ever take the risk of loving me? I'm not lovable, so I'd better not make the mistake of falling in love with someone else only to let them reject me." Children who neglect their appearance, stop spending time with friends, withdraw to their rooms, and fail to return affectionate overtures gives evidence of this fear. A parent might use "a hypothetical situation" in an attempt to probe for this type of underlying thought. "I once heard of a child," the parent might say, "who had a favorite best friend, but one summer the best friend moved away. This child started to feel. . . ." And the parent describes the feelings of being unlovable. If it is a true reflection of the child's feelings, he or she might either experience vicarious comfort or raise questions about particular elements of the experience.

Contacts with Two Nuclear Families

For the most part, it is mothers who are awarded custody of their children following divorce. In fact, the one child in ten not assigned to the mother's household post-divorce is less likely to be assigned to the father's household than to some other living arrangement like other relatives, foster homes, or institutions (Belsky, Lerner, and Spanier, 1984). With the small percentage of actual father custody, it is child support and visitation that is their likely role. Currently, only one divorced father in six sees his children at least once a week (Furstenberg et al., 1983). Another one in six visits at least once a month. The majority of fathers see their children less than once a year after divorce, though I would venture that these statistics change yearly. With this great a variation in parental contact, it should follow that the experience of parental divorce across children is highly variable. It is only recently that commentary on divorce has acknowledged that the pre-divorce relationships between children and parents, particularly fathers, also span the entire range from barely existent through conflicted or ambivalent to cherished. Some families, therefore, must encourage children after divorce to seek an active love from people who are present and available, some must assist children in designing and maintaining a long-distance father–child relationship, and some must cope with the demands created by the specifics of visitation. In addition, those families in which the father retains custody find themselves on uncharted ground since there are few models to follow in both custody and visitation. We will know more about the unique features of father-custody families in another ten years.

Whatever the custody and visitation arrangement, children themselves crave meaningful contact with each parent and some manner of ongoing relationship with their father and mother. Current thinking on divorce as a process suggests that divorce does not *end* a relationship as much as it *changes* a relationship, particularly when former spouses share children in common (Stark, 1986). The former triad of mother–father–child becomes a new constellation of two nuclear families, binuclear if you will.

On the one hand, the adults must attempt to subdue their own emotional reactions to the severed spousal relationship in order for the child to continue successful relations with both parents. To prevent ill effects for the child and for both mother–child and father–child relations, the visitation arrangements should occur on time, with the child prepared to anticipate both leaving and returning without judgment or malice. There are many losers in the game of visitation revenge when one parent attempts to hoard the child's love by being too indulgent with the child, too critical of the other parent, or too uncooperative in meeting the regulations of the visitation agreement.

On the other hand, it is the child who must in fact find the ability to cope in two family settings. One preschool boy in joint custody lived alternating months in towns two hundred miles apart. Besides two families, two houses, and two sets of relatives, he developed neighborhood friends and day care classmates in each town. It is important to acknowledge that it is the child who must draw on personal resources in order to find a niche in each setting and cope with the transitions between the two. And children will differ in their ability to do so.

As in other situations of distress, a child might construct defenses with regard to visitation. Just as a child might feign illness on school days when progress in school seems blocked by perceived failures, one child might feel sick on visitation days. Another might regress to age-inappropriate behavior. Another child persuasively might enroll in a high-status activity that just happens to conflict with visitation times. Still another might begin to assault the custodial parent as the anxiety escalates before and after each visit. All these children are signaling that they do not yet have the strength to cope realistically with this newest demand. In the absence of an effective strategy for understanding the changes, the child uses artificial defenses to help contain the anxiety generated by the unknown.

The parent who wishes to aid the child would do well to avoid taking issue with the actual expression of the anxiety. The undesirable behavior is a signal that there is too much anxiety for the child to control and that something must change. Either the demands of the situation must change, or the child's adaptive skills must increase. To change the situation, one might invite the child's best friend along during a visitation excursion, take cassette tapes of the custodial parent reading a favorite bedtime story, or find places in the new neighborhood that would be of particular interest to the child. To help increase the child's coping skills, one might model brief but effective relaxation strategies, encourage the child to pack his/her latest project to work on, or read stories of children who have found new strength and courage in their own lives.

The bottom line is that every child has the right to a loving relationship with each parent, regardless of the state of the relationship between the once-married adults. Those children fortunate enough to have parents who speak well of their former spouse and who indicate that they value the qualities of both sexes are children who overcome the crisis of divorce most readily (Hetherington, Cox, and Cox, 1978). It is a matter of personal integrity for former spouses to differentiate parental qualities from spousal qualities in their own minds before engaging in discussions with their children regarding the ex-spouse.

On a more personal note, I believe this investment of effort in maintaining the integrity of the former spouse is particularly crucial in this era when more fathers are voluntarily and heartily participating in childbirth and child rearing. It must be a great sorrow to be a parent, mother or father, attached to a child in ways that only mothers once were, facing the realization of being without that child on a day-to-day basis. Those fathers who take steps to be attentive, nurturant, and involved as parents face major adjustments if their marriages move to divorce and the mother is assigned custody of the children. For children to succeed in maintaining close and meaningful relations with both such parents, each parent must be committed to facilitating their child's relationship with the other. One would hope that creative and compassionate solutions will be found in the contemporary family's search for post-divorce parent–child relationships.

Positive Grounding in Antagonistic Circumstances

In reality, some portion of families must deal with situations in which one or both parents contrive to win the favor of their children at the expense of their ex-spouse. They make statements that are clearly indicative of bitter, angry, hostile, resentful, and hateful feelings toward the other. They use methods that are spiteful, vengeful, mean, and full of sabotage to downgrade the ex-spouse. The victims of this ill-will are often trapped by their powerlessness to deflect the malice that is emitted. Under such treatment, one would surely choose to construct a reality that helps avoid contact with the antagonistic person.

I am struck by the fact that committed parents attempt to endure the ongoing conflict in an effort to maintain any relationship at all with their children. Many parents in these circumstances will mention that it is particularly tempting to consider stepping out of the picture altogether. Their greatest fear is that the vengeful parent will retaliate against the children and make their lives miserable when they display loyalty and affection to the victimized ex-spouse. One other possible scenario is that of a parent misconstruing the other's words and actions in reports to children, making children unloved, unwanted, and mistreated by the victimized parent. When it is the custodial parent who does so, an added weapon is informing children that the visitation-only parent has "no right" to influence them, even in simple matters like house rules, curfew, and bedtime, against their wishes. Overcoming these continuous threats to the parent–child relationship seems like an insurmountable task to accomplish when the contact is only occasional at best.

But I think it can be done. This is such a serious matter that it requires a societal response. It is common knowledge that certain lawyers advocate an adversarial relationship in divorce cases in order to gain a better settlement for their own clients. This often results, however, in affirming and perpetuating antagonistic interactions. I would like to see the legal community support protection from victimization between ex-spouses in their relationships with their children. I believe that schools can help educate children to the realities of the human condition, including the many faces of love, the complexity of adult choices, and the dangers of unilateral power. When a beloved parent contrives to influence a child for good or ill, the message is highly persuasive, particularly if the child is too young to reason through it independently. It is possible, however, to raise the consciousness of children to these issues by open discussions among classmates in schools. Perhaps those students who have previously experienced antagonism as objectionable will be more likely to withstand such threats to the integrity of their relationship with the victimized parent. In the best of all scenarios, the child might even raise his or her objections to the antagonistic parent, admonishing them to be "fair" instead.

My advice to parents currently experiencing this inhumane treatment is to communicate with children in ways that attempt to provide the larger perspective on human nature, including, but not limited to, the elements of conflict. In most instances it would be ineffective to try to "win" the power play set up by the antagonistic parent. Stepping into the power struggle only serves to intensify the other's efforts to dominate and subvert. It is through redefining the task that one surmounts the threat posed by the assault and vilification. Trying to accomplish this without resorting to the same methods of defamation requires a fine balance.

"People who are angry," a woman might say to a child in response to a father's accusation that she is an unfit mother, "think only of a person's faults and failings and not of their admirable qualities. In reality every person has strengths and weaknesses, including me." "Sometimes adults find that they have to face impossible choices," a man might say to a child in response to a mother's accusation that he abandoned his children, "choices in situations where no compromise is possible. If both choices are desirable or both are undesirable, adults ask themselves which one of the two they are capable of living with."

Each of these responses removes the victimized parent from the danger of escalating the win–lose power struggle. Each turns the personal affront into a commentary on the human condition. Each transcends the specific case and instance by generalizing to the whole of humanity. Each gives the child information he or she can utilize in comparable situations. Children differ, of course, in their ability to absorb and apply these insights. But one might suspect that children who are exposed to this type of commentary would be more likely to bring such thinking to bear on the problems in their own lives.

In the rare instance where the child is coached by the antagonistic parent to counter every humane initiative by the victimized parent, stronger strategies are necessary. "It is a disservice to you," a man might say to a child in response to a mother who insists that the courts have given her power to determine the child's best interests, "to have you think that the laws of court are the only laws that bind people. There is the law of the heart as well. You know in your heart and I know in my heart that I am your dad. That is a fact that no one can change. And because I am your dad, I will have feelings for you and wishes for you and goals for you, regardless of the ruling of the courts. I will continue to trust and hope that the moment will come when I am free to act on those wishes. But until then, the knowledge that you exist in the world as a child of mine gives me great joy." As in all the examples reported here, it is not the exact words that matter as much as the message of love and caring and parental concern.

With these strategies as foundations, I would support parents who strive to maintain contact with their children at great personal cost. While they might feel powerless to counter the vehemence of the antagonistic parent's wrath, they may be able to provide some element of positive grounding for their children as they live through such unfortunate circumstances. Perhaps their insights will only become meaningful as the child matures. But without their efforts, there might be no moderating influence at all to balance out the antagonism that children witness.

Loss of Contact

It is also important for us to acknowledge that some parents of divorce choose not to maintain contact with their children. Either by intent or by default, they are physically and psychologically unavailable to their children. What makes the issue more complex is that it is not always a lack of love that results in so dramatic an outcome. Some parents feel so wrenched by repeating their good-byes on a weekly basis that they decide to lessen their pain by diminishing contact. Some parents are so acutely aware of the devious ways their ex-spouses use the visitation arrangement to manipulate the children that they choose to avoid contact in order to reduce the conflict to which their children are exposed.

However the rift occurs, some children must deal with the reality that a parent will not be a part of their lives. Try as they might, wish as they might, the decision on maintaining contact is under adult control. Human nature what it is, it is clearly easier not to make plans than to make plans, thus many opportunities for visitation simply do not occur. In many families, child support, not visitation, is the topic of concern (Nuta, 1986). Half of all the child support bills are not paid in full. Family scholars are only beginning to unravel the multiple influences in effect here.

In the case of an absent parent, it might be best to assist the child in transforming the active love to a memory love (Bloom, 1967). Families that are single parent structured because of the death of a spouse typically rely on memory love to serve as a continuing influence of the absent parent. Children are exhorted to perfect skills and accomplish tasks because the deceased parent would have wished it so. Some of the means surviving parents use to comfort and socialize the child can be adapted for those situations of divorce in which a parent ceases contact with a child. Supportive comments might focus on the good fortune of having had as many years together as there were, the ways in which the child continues to be like the absent parent, the pride the absent parent would feel if they knew of the child's accomplishments, and the legacy to love others as well as the child feels he or she was once loved by the absent parent. The important element here is that active longing and grieving hurts. If the love is viewed instead as memories, those memories can be replayed at will, giving solace in their repetition. One might, for example, vow to attend more fireworks displays because of a particularly happy night once spent enjoying fireworks with the absent parent.

Even books written specifically for children whose parents are divorced insist that, just as no one can get blood from a stone, so no one can manufacture love where it is not available (Gardner, 1983). The custodial parent who seeks a perspective for explaining such a situation to a child would do well to reflect on the resolution scene from *Ordinary People.* "She loved you as well as she was able, no more and no less" (Guest, 1976). We cannot second guess the mystery of another person's love. But we can monitor the love we hold and the love we share, acknowledging that it is a gift freely given from one who is capable of giving to one who is capable of receiving. When cherished myths are replaced with realistic appraisal, children are encouraged to build a well-grounded structure for the loves in their own lives.

Impact Beyond the Family

Counselors often caution an adult contemplating divorce that the event will transform every existing relationship, not just those with spouse and children. One becomes estranged from in-laws, disjoined from religious affiliation, less welcome to socialize with groups of couples, and appraised at risk by school authorities. One school-age boy in a town of 36,000 announced to his parents that he was the only one in his class of twenty-six whose parents had never divorced.

Remarriage is certainly one resolution to the anguish of divorce (Wallerstein and Kelly, 1980). However, it is increasingly likely that such remarriages involve blended families, that is the blending of mates with children from prior marriages, along with children shared in common. The increase in number of stepparents, step-brothers, stepsisters, half-brothers, and half-sisters is changing the complexion of the American family in contemporary society. Legal, economic, educational, and recreational practices are strained to keep pace with the new advances.

Functioning as a Team

Whether death, divorce, unwed status, or adoptive status produces the single parent family, the reality of life for one adult and child or children is one that involves one less contributing member compared to dual parent families. The single head of household attempts to perform or satisfy all the functions of family living fulfilled by dual parent families. As summarized by Goldberg and Deutsch (1977), these include legal, economic, educational, recreational, affiliative, and socialization functions. Health, safety, and welfare are elements of the legal function. Provisions for food, clothing, and shelter are elements of the economic function. Love, tenderness, and belonging are elements of the affiliative function. All manner of teaching a child to be a participating member of a specific society are elements of the socialization function.

While divorce itself has come to be viewed as a temporary crisis that family members seem to weather in a period of approximately two years (Hetherington, 1980), life in a single parent household often involves some inherent conditions which prove to be disrupting over a long period of time. As one adult attempts to shoulder the responsibilities once shared by two, some of the tasks are bound to be left unmet. It seems to be the question of the 1980s—how to hold a job, raise children, keep a house, entertain friends, learn something new, contribute to charities, and find time for oneself all in the course of a twenty-four-hour day. The added challenge for the single head of household is how to guarantee that the critical functions are met in some ways. What is important is streamlining the task load by ignoring some nonessential tasks without deteriorating into disorganization and unpredictability. Unmade beds and fewer elaborate meals do not put family members at risk.

Without support from adult friends and relatives or children old enough to participate in family affairs, one sole parent is stretched to the limit attempting to meet these challenges. In fact, divorce often results in two single parent families stretched to the limit by the solitary demands. One way to ease the strain is to be able to afford to purchase the needed services (Belsky, Lerner, and Spanier, 1984). Another is to develop a network of social supports through friends, counselors, and parent-support groups to help provide the instrumental and emotional assistance needed. The assistance given by significant other adults is a safeguard against a diminishing quality of life, whether the others be relatives, friends, lovers, neighbors, colleagues, or other single parents. One mother whose own children were away at college invited her friend's preschool son for an afternoon of ice-skating. In addition to the relief provided for the single parent, the boy had the good fortune of establishing a personal relationship with another caring adult. Concerned friends and social service providers might benefit from the literature now available on life in single parent families (Schlesinger, 1986).

Minimizing Disruptions

In the midst of sorting through essential and nonessential tasks, the maintenance of a semblance of routine and organization helps families through the transition period. Despite emotional distress, despite self-preoccupation, despite changes in residence, despite the fatigue of new demands, the anticipation and follow-through of expected routines lends some familiarity in the face of the unknown. It is not the maintenance of the pre-divorce lifestyle that is critical for children here; it is the security of the continuation of sensitive parenting. There are, in fact, many strategies available for reducing the burden while still meeting the demands. Meals prepared on weekends to be reheated during the week preserve the family dinner hour without overloading the single parent in the hour after work. A cassette tape of the parent reading a favorite bedtime story can give welcome respite at the end of a particularly tiring day. Inviting a neighborhood friend on a trip to the playground provides a playmate for a child, leaving one time to read the newspaper or chat with a friend. Children thrive on the continuity of expected routines. Children who make the best adjustments after divorce have parents who preserve the favored routines, even if they are simplified to reflect the realities of available time and energy (Hetherington, 1980).

Shift in Responsibilities

The single parent who faces the challenge of fulfilling family functions alone thus seems to have four options from which to choose. He or she can attempt to meet all the needs by working harder, eliminate some of them and hope they don't disadvantage the child, find participating adults to share some of the responsibility, or train the children to do some of the tasks. It is well-documented that children in single parent families have responsibility for more of the household tasks that children in dual parent families (Hetherington, 1980). For example, they learn to do laundry and help cook family meals at younger ages. The parent who arranges this shift in responsibilities by emphasizing each person's contributions to teamwork in the family achieves three goals: reducing one's own workload so one is not overburdened, defining the workload that is involved in raising and caring for a family, and training children in the accomplishment of the tasks. We would hypothesize that children holding responsibility for reasonable household tasks through childhood show greater facility in accomplishing these tasks as adults than children without such training. We might even raise the conjecture that boys who receive this childhood training become husbands willing and able to cooperate in dispensing with household chores.

There is one pitfall, however, in children possibly growing to dislike and avoid housekeeping tasks in any form, almost as a reaction against this early responsibility. When children are required to adjust to, say, father leaving, mother working, changing schools, *and* increased responsibilities at home, it is easy to see how the household chores could take on negative overtones. But when the request for assistance is balanced with attention and gratitude, the result is likely to be pride in accomplishment.

Dealing with Times of Stress

Many families, both dual parent families and single parent families, experience difficult and demanding moments of extreme strain. When a child encounters academic difficulties, a teen expresses emotional distress through antisocial behavior, a parent encounters financial difficulties or becomes ill, or when an elderly parent becomes dependent, adults are often hard-pressed to find solutions while they meet their other responsibilities. The single parent is particularly strained to marshal the reserves to meet one more crisis. Some difficulties can be resolved through a process of observation, reanalysis, and intervention. In attempting to deal with childhood stress, one must first observe to identify the situations which produce stress for the child and note the child's reactions (Doyle, Gold, and Moskowitz, 1984). In the reanalysis stage, one must consider the dilemma from the child's perspective, guessing how a child might interpret and react to the various features of the situation. That information can be used to design an intervention by changing something within the situation. Perhaps a private spot for studies is needed. Perhaps some assertiveness training can help the child field remarks from classmates. Perhaps a plan to earn a desired object by assisting an elderly grandparent could be implemented. Each of these strategies can be developed and applied without turning to formal sources for intervention.

When it is the parent who is incapacitated through illness, hospitalization, overtime, or personal distress, children need an alternate arrangement for care. No one night of dimmed lights and peanut butter sandwiches will harm a child. But children need adult supervision in times of continuing unavailability of the parent. Depending on age and maturity, older children in the family can take charge by following the parent's instructions, as in other cultures. But the best solution is training children to seek care from one trusted adult friend of the family. That adult might be a relative, a neighbor, a co-worker, the parent of a classmate, a family from church, or a representative from a social service agency. Children learn and practice how to reach that adult in times of need. Some school districts have begun to identify "block parents" who have agreed to assist children whose parents aren't available after school. The more dependable the social network, the better prepared the single parent family will be for coping in times of stress.

In some circumstances, the stress is likely to be ongoing but situational. There is evidence that parents of handicapped children are more likely to divorce than parents of non-handicapped children (Schilling et al., 1986). The same applies for parents whose children have been victimized. The life situation that burdened two parents is yet more burdensome for one parent alone. To manage under these circumstances one might search first for available community resources to provide assistance. One might share living arrangements with another family, obtaining both instrumental and emotional assistance. Or one might participate in a parent-support group composed of other adults facing similar situations in their own lives.

Whatever arrangement is made, it is critical for the custodial parent to have some private time with other adults and for each sibling to have time with friends and with each parent that is not devoted to care.

Ongoing Socialization

The process of socialization is dynamic rather than static, changing over time as both parent and children grow and change. With the child's increases in physical, cognitive, and socio-emotional skills, his or her reactions to a parent's socialization practices change. It is the parent's role to adjust their demands accordingly, using the child's new talents in the service of progress toward maturity. The child, for example, who comes to perceive that others have different points of view can help plan a birthday party for a younger sibling. At the same time, however, these developing skills lead a child into new and uncharted territory whose pitfalls parents must anticipate. As children come to perceive that peers have goals different from parents, they begin to conform to the actions of peers. It is the reciprocal nature of socialization that is the hallmark of parent–child relations (Bell and Harper, 1977). In single parent families one adult alone faces the demands of initiating and reacting with children in the process of socialization. The critical point here is that the strategies continue to change as parents and children change. What worked before single parent status may not work now simply because development itself raises the need for change. And change must come from the awareness of one parent rather than from the joint perspectives of two parents.

Trust, Communication, and Guidance

Current research indicates that sons are more likely than daughters to have difficulty coping with the impact of divorce (Hetherington, 1980). Sons, as well as daughters, are most likely to be raised in mother-headed households following divorce. One possible explanation, therefore, is that cross-sex single parenting is not as facilitative as same-sex single parenting. Though the data on father-custody families are scarce, there is an indication that fathers raising sons are more successful than fathers raising daughters alone (Santrock, Warshak, and Elliot, 1982).

 Single mothers raising sons are most likely to experience strain if they are highly authoritative, set inflexible rules, and deliver more criticism and punishment for rule-breaking than praise for desirable behavior. Children of all ages and all life circumstances develop self-regulation of mature behavior when a parent is warm and affectionate, sets age-appropriate expectations, and discusses the experience of events with them (Santrock, Warshak, and Elliot, 1982).

Buffered by this parental warmth and ongoing communication attempts, youths are likely to relate to and imitate the words and actions of such a parent. By contrast, one result of harsh, power-dominated discipline by parents is the decision by teens to remain absent from the house for long periods of time. Since parents can influence an absent teen less than one who is present, positive guidance and caring serves to guarantee that parental admonitions fall on fertile ground.

The question for examination here is that of how a single parent might act to maintain communication with youths while the whole fabric of the family is wrenched and shifted. For years now, child-rearing scholars have underscored the value of consistency in parental behavior toward children. When there is upheaval in all one's life circumstances, consistency seems to be a long lost treasure. It is possible, however, to be consistent in one's "philosophy" about children, childhood, and child rearing even in the midst of multiple changes. One can continue to uphold and act upon certain vital beliefs regardless of changing circumstances, beliefs like all children having rights to the same respect one would accord to adults, all children seeking organizing principles which help them make sense out of the realities they encounter, all children having the capacity for and tendency toward positive healthy functioning even though it might be strained at times by life's challenges, etc. I would argue that behavior based on such beliefs would be comforting to all children, regardless of the match or mismatch to prior experience in the pre-divorce family.

Preparation for Adulthood

There is every good chance that children who have been deftly guided through the swift currents of the journey from dual parent family to single parent family, and perhaps back again, have indeed learned invaluable lessons for their own adulthood. It is my deep regret that we do so little in our society to educate our youths to the differences between loving, being in love, having a relationship, and building an enduring relationship. Raised in stable, intact families, they typically see few of the processes and strategies inherent in such adult decisions.

Maybe, just maybe, the children of today who are audience to changing adult relationships will be better schooled on the nature of love and love relationships. We do know that they spend more time giving thought and consideration to the question of family itself than do children who are "spared" the pain of parental divorce (Wallerstein and Kelly, 1980). They see more of the stages of the process of love than do children whose parents remain at the stage of conjugal love. They observe while a single parent engages in dating, mate selection, courtship, marriage, and possible dual-city households. Here they have the opportunity to witness the search for love, love in the making, love under test, and love capable of withstanding time and distance. Perhaps those children who have learned to function well in a single parent family by finding strength within themselves and support around them will grow to be adults who understand that they are capable of designing enduring relationships which are not threatened by the ravages of time and circumstance. In living with caring and resourceful single parents, they might come to value the forthright and loving natures of the important adults in their lives and identify with those qualities in their own adult lives. Future research will help us test the accuracy of this compelling hypothesis.

References

BELL, R. Q. and R. V. Harper. *Child Effects on Adults.* Hillsdale, NJ:Erlbaum (1977).

BELSKY, J., R. M. Lerner, and G. B. Spanier. *The Child in the Family.* Reading, MA:Addison-Wesley (1984).

BLOOM, M. "Toward a Developmental Concept of Love," *Journal of Human Relations,* 15:246–263 (1967).

CARLSON, J. S. "Cross-Cultural Piagetian Studies: What Can They Tell Us?" in *The Developing Individual in a Changing World,* K. F. Riegel and J. A. Meacham, eds., Chicago:Aldine (1976).

ELKIND, D. and R. Bowen. "Imaginary Audience Behavior in Children and Adolescents," *Developmental Psychology,* 15:38–44 (1979).

FURSTENBERG, F., C. Nord, J. Peterson, and N. Zill. "The Life Course of Children of Divorce: Marital Disruption and Parental Contact," *American Sociological Review* (1983).

GARDNER, R. A. *The Boys and Girls Book About One-Parent Families.* New York:Bantam Books (1983).

GELMAN, R. "The Nature and Development of Early Number Concepts," in *Advances in Child Development and Behavior,* Vol. 7, H. W. Reese, ed., New York:Academic Press (1972).

GOLDBERG, S. R. and F. Deutsch. *Lifespan Individual and Family Development.* Monterey, CA:Brooks/Cole (1977).

GREENFIELD, P. M. "Cross-Cultural Research and Piagetian Theory: Paradox and Progress," in *The Developing Individual in a Changing World*, K. F. Riegel and J. A. Meacham, eds., Chicago:Aldine (1976).

HETHERINGTON, E. M. "Children and Divorce," in *Parent Child Interaction: Theory, Research and Prospect*, R. Henderson, ed., New York:Academic Press (1980).

HETHERINGTON, E. M., M. Cox, and R. Cox. "The Development of Children in Mother-Headed Families," in *The American Family: Dying or Developing*, H. Hoffman and D. Reiss, eds., New York:Plenum (1978).

MAHLER, M. S., F. Pine, and A. Bergman. *The Psychological Birth of the Human Infant: Symbiosis and Individuation*. New York:Basic Books (1975).

NUTA, V. R. "Emotional Aspects of Child Support Enforcement," *Family Relations*, 35(1):177–181 (1986).

PIAGET, J. *The Construction of Reality in the Child*. New York:Basic Books (1954).

PIAGET, J. *The Language and Thought of the Child*. Cleveland, OH:World Publishing Co. (1955).

PIAGET, J. *Judgment and Reasoning in the Child*. Totowa, NJ:Littlefield, Adams & Co. (1959).

PIAGET, J. *The Child's Conception of Physical Causality*. Totowa, NJ:Littlefield, Adams & Co. (1960).

PIAGET, J. *The Child's Conception of Time*. New York:Basic Books (1970).

PIAGET, J. and B. Inhelder. *The Child's Conception of Space*. New York:Norton (1967).

SANTROCK, J., R. Warshak, and G. Elliot. "Social Development and Parent–Child Interaction in Father-Custody and Stepmother Families," in *Nontraditional Families*, M. Lamb, ed., Hillsdale, NJ:Erlbaum (1982).

SCHLESINGER, B. "Single Parent Families: A Bookshelf, 1978–1985," *Family Relations*, 35(1):199–204 (1986).

STARK, E. "Friends Through It All," *Psychology Today*, 20(5):54–60 (1986).

WALLERSTEIN, J. S. and J. B. Kelly. *Surviving the Breakup: How Children and Parents Cope with Divorce*. New York:Basic Books (1980).

CHAPTER 6

Addressing Special Learning Needs of Single Parent Children

MARTHA J. LALLY
SUSAN L. TROSTLE

Introduction

A CENTURY AGO a number of influential people labeled "divorce conservatives" attempted to publicize the connection between the rapidly emerging divorce phenomenon and the deterioration of the family. The conservatives contended that divorce "involved an apparent conflict between the public welfare and individual rights" (O'Neill, 1967). Divorce, it was feared, was weakening the most important foundation of society . . . the family. "Society is doomed," the conservatives lamented, as divorce rates steadily increased and, simultaneously, individualism gained widespread popularity.

Individual rights began to achieve a great deal of recognition in the late nineteenth and early twentieth centuries. Increasingly, husbands and wives were unwilling to live with the costs of their spouses' unfilled obligations. Common causes for divorce and separation, for example, included husband's alcoholism, and so-called "nonmaternal" wives (May, 1980).

After 1900, however, "individualism" was expressed for different reasons. Now, couples frequently sought more rewards in their lives; they were not seeking divorce merely to escape costs (May, 1980). Men, for example, sought wives who were exciting as well as virtuous; women expected their mates to be fun-loving as well as good providers. Today, financially secure women between the ages of thirty and forty are, increasingly, choosing to bear or adopt children as single parents or while cohabitating with persons of the same or opposite sex (Salholz, 1986).

The complicating factor in this new quest "is inevitably children" (Scanzoni, 1983). In the past the family functioned as an economic, academic, and social unit. Education transpired primarily in the home. The family was responsible for helping children acquire many complex language, comprehension, and problem-solving skills. As the children were involved in productive and meaningful family tasks, they learned important skills, values, and attitudes (Bartolome, 1982). Parent and child interaction was constant and continued as they worked to maintain and support the nuclear family.

The Single Parent Family

Today the single parent family, as well as industrialization in our society, have changed the emotional, social, and economic functions of the family. In its quest for "individualism," children in nontraditional families have become isolated from the worlds of work, their community and, many times, from their relations and friends. No longer is parenting a shared responsibility. Families are increasingly struggling to become self-sufficient.

Regardless of the self-sufficient individualism currently pervading modern society, Kenniston (1977) argued that families cannot function in isolation:

> The myth of self-sufficiency blinds us to the workings of other forces in family life. For families are not now, nor were they ever, the self-sufficient building blocks of society exclusively responsible, praiseworthy, and blamable for their own destiny. They were deeply influenced by broad social and economic forces over which they have little control [p. 12].

Isolation of the single parent from relatives and other support groups may pose serious threats to the single parent's children. "Young children, innocent victims of divorce, learn to perceive themselves as abandoned misfits and residuals of a perfect lifestyle, the stereotyped two parent family" (Whitfield and Freeland, 1982, p. 19).

The Child with Learning Needs

For the purposes of this chapter, a learning need is defined as a disorder in understanding or using spoken or written language. At home, behavioral evidence of learning deficiencies include: (a) difficulty following directions, (b) poor peer/sibling relationships, (c) frequent testing of limits, and (d) short attention span for most tasks.

At school, manifestations of learning needs include problems in reading, writing, spelling, and arithmetic. The definition includes learning disabled children, as well as children commonly labeled "slow learner," "developmentally delayed," or "environmentally deprived."

As many as half the nation's children, over 3.2 million, will at some time in their lives like in a "broken home." Of this number, more than 13 percent, or 416,000 children will be labeled "exceptional" in the schools (LeMasters, 1974; Zintl and Thomas, 1986). The classification of "exceptional" includes gifted, mentally retarded, physically handicapped, and emotionally troubled, as well as learning disabled and slow learning children (Lefrancois, 1983; LeMasters, 1974). For single parent children who may lack economic and environmental advantages, the proportion of those encountering special learning needs and other problems requiring referral dramatically increase (Lefrancois, 1983).

The presence of a child with learning needs in a single parent family poses an additional severe challenge to both the parent and the child. The emotional well-being of the parent affects the child's emotional state, which, in turn can facilitate the child's learning processes and academic achievement (Hetherington, 1982).

Figure 6.1 illustrates the relationship among the parent's emotional state and the child's well-being and resultant ultimate performance (starting point is optional).

The single parent frequently feels overwhelmed by the emotional demands instigated by: (a) lack of social support; (b) financial con-

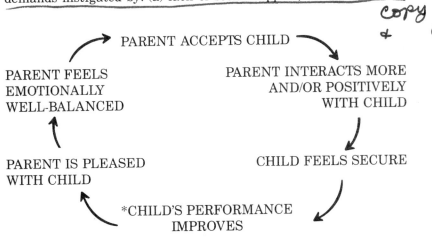

PARENT ACCEPTS CHILD

PARENT FEELS EMOTIONALLY WELL-BALANCED

PARENT INTERACTS MORE AND/OR POSITIVELY WITH CHILD

PARENT IS PLEASED WITH CHILD

CHILD FEELS SECURE

*CHILD'S PERFORMANCE IMPROVES

* Starting point is optional.

Figure 6.1. Single parent facilitative cycle.

straints; or (c) increased responsibilities (Love, 1970). The added challenge of rearing a child with special learning needs may perpetuate a dysfunctional cycle similar to the illustration in Figure 6.2.

The facilitation and dysfunctional cycles suggest that the single parent is an especially dominant influence in the emotional and academic development of the "at risk" child. Parents, in general, are in the best position to coordinate and assume the long-term responsibilities for interventions aimed at maximizing the developmental potential of the child. Learning programs involving parents substantially enhance the child's cognitive development and produce more enduring effects than interventions that do not involve the parent (Bronfenbrenner, 1979). The provision of outside resources and programs, thus, is especially appropriate and recommended for the single parent (Bronfenbrenner, 1974).

Single parents of children with learning needs may require assistance from these programs in three dimensions (McWhirter, 1980):

(1) Cognitive: The parent needs facts and information.
(2) Affective: The parent needs assistance in dealing with the emotional issues resulting from having a child with learning needs.
(3) Psycho-motor: The parent needs to have both the facts and the resulting feelings recognized and addressed in an action-oriented, individualized program.

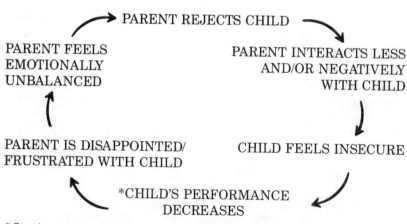

PARENT REJECTS CHILD

PARENT FEELS EMOTIONALLY UNBALANCED

PARENT INTERACTS LESS AND/OR NEGATIVELY WITH CHILD

PARENT IS DISAPPOINTED/ FRUSTRATED WITH CHILD

CHILD FEELS INSECURE

*CHILD'S PERFORMANCE DECREASES

* Starting point is optional.

Figure 6.2. Single parent dysfunctional cycle.

Detecting Learning Problems

If a single parent suspects his/her child of having a learning need, professional assistance is sought (a) to obtain information and (b) to ascertain whether there is, in fact, a learning problem. Three major steps are taken:

(1) Contact the pediatrician or a health clinic. Arrange to have a complete physical examination of the child to detect or rule out any physical problems or sight and hearing loss. If needed, the physician refers the child to another specialist for a more detailed examination.

(2) Make a complete developmental history. The history includes details about the pregnancy and birth, childhood diseases or accidents, behavior problems, eating and sleeping habits, medications, and so on. This record aids in diagnosing the problem.

(3) Contact community agencies. A contact to agencies specializing in learning needs children is made; information about children's learning problems and special programs existing in the area is available. These agencies may also provide information concerning parent organizations that help a single parent better deal with a learning problem child.

If these steps are achieved and the single parent continues to have concerns about the child, the parent can initiate plans to have the child tested for possible learning disabilities. If the child is not yet in school, several alternatives are available:

(1) The local Health Department may sponsor programs that offer diagnostic testing and child education/evaluation services, and supply information about preschool programs for children with learning needs.

(2) Some hospitals provide a team of specialists who work together to test and evaluate children and recommend interventions to assist with the learning problem.

(3) The local school system may offer a preschool special services program that evaluates children not yet in kindergarten.

If the preschool child is found to have a learning need, the law guarantees special education services for children at three years of age or older.   O -3 now

Typically, children are not referred for a learning evaluation until they are in school. The teacher usually refers the school-aged child with special learning needs. Once referred, a multidisciplinary team is required by law to review the referral and administer a comprehensive evaluation if determined necessary. The tests and other evaluation materials need to be administered in the child's natural language; they must not be socially or culturally discriminatory. The tests are also tailored to assess specific areas or educational needs and not designed merely to provide a single general intelligence quotient. Areas of assessment and commonly used individually administered tests used during an evaluation for children suspected of having a learning problem are listed in Appendix A at the conclusion of this chapter.

The multidisciplinary team and parents need to reach agreement about the findings of the evaluation. If the child is found to have a learning need and a special education placement is recommended, an Individual Educational Program (IEP) is developed and implemented. The IEP is a written agreement among all parties clearly stating what will be provided for the child.

According to P.L. 94-142 (Education for all Handicapped Children Act, 1975), special education children are taught in the least restrictive environment. A special or separate classroom is considered only when placement in a regular class is inappropriate. Children are placed in programs based on the severity of their disability. A given child's program may be changed as long as a new IEP meeting is held. At this meeting the parent discusses the child's IEP for the following academic year with the special education teacher. A child's program may also be changed after a three-year reevaluation is completed (as stated by P. L. 94-142).

Dealing with Emotional Reactions

Emotional reactions commonly experienced by single parents of learning-needs children include: (a) confusion, (b) self-blame, (c) loss of self-control, (d) frustration, (e) anger, (f) scapegoating, (g) intolerance, (h) unpreparedness, (i) defensiveness, and (j) rejection (Vigilante, 1983).

Single parents of children with learning needs are, understandably, often bewildered and confused about the child's problems (McWhirter, 1980). Professionals, too, are confused as to the etiology, identification, and teaching strategies of these special needs children.

The parent may experience self-blame for a real or imagined personal weakness which is believed, genetically or environmentally, to have contributed to a child's learning problem (Vigilante, 1983). The child's problem, however, is not necessarily the parent's fault. No single cause for children's learning problems exists. More often a complex interaction of causes is responsible, including brain damage or other neurological impairment, various diseases and infections, malnutrition, and other environmental, genetic, motivational, or readiness factors (Lefrancois, 1983). Self-blame may increase parental stress, further interfering with the parent's ability to assist the child. Further, the energy requirement of guilt often becomes overwhelming for the parent.

As a consequence of the frustrating nature of the child's learning needs, single parents often undergo a loss of self-control (Vigilante, 1983). They may feel overwhelmed or helpless.

Likewise, self-control in the child with learning problems may require a significantly longer period of time to develop since the developmental process is often hindered. Thus, single parents must learn how to deal with their own feelings of losing control, while at the same time, helping the child gain self-control (see Figure 6.1).

These emotional reactions are further compounded by confusion and bewilderment with accompanying frustration (McWhirter, 1980). The child's inconsistent behavior often increases frustration. Parental responses to frustration are many and varied. The goal is to channel the frustration into positive action, e.g., recognizing the nature of the difficulty, that progress may be slow, and that patience and quality-time-on-task are required.

A parent may experience anger and hostility toward the child with special needs (McWhirter, 1980). If the child is the target of the anger, the child's problems become aggravated and remediation is more difficult (see Figure 6.2). Single parents, who learn to vent their anger through profitable outlets such as structuring the environment and creative problem solving experience lessened feelings of hostility and resentfulness.

Blaming the ex-husband or -wife, other family members, doctors, school personnel, and others dealing with the child is another form of expressing anger (McWhirter, 1980). Scapegoating of this sort isolates the parent from potentially helpful sources, obviously interfering with the needed cooperation among parent, family, and those professionals serving the child.

It is not uncommon for a parent to become intolerant of the child with learning problems (McWhirter, 1980). Since a child with learning needs is normal in many respects, a parent may direct pressure on the child; however, the pressure may be unreasonable, given the constraints of the problem. For example, the parent may require the child to respond immediately to an instruction and then resent the child's inability to respond as quickly as one might expect.

Similarly, the parent may impatiently (and unreasonably) pressure the professional for the educational, medical, or psychological treatment that will lead to "complete" normalcy. This is referred to as the "Taste of Honey" phenomenon (McCarthy and McCarthy, 1969). The "honey" of progress toward normalcy may be experienced by gains made through advice by professionals. Once such gains are experienced the parent may demand greater gains and expect them to occur more quickly.

The constructive reaction is the recognition that gains are made slowly and sometimes tediously by both educators and parent. The parents who build their interactions and efforts with the child on the strengths of their child will find that their initial intolerance and pressure are redirected into more constructive channels.

Single parents are frequently unprepared for the role of dealing single-handedly with a child who has learning needs. They may be unable to meet the expectations of professionals. Despite good intentions, they may over-control, over-protect, over-indulge, or, generally, over-baby the child. The child's development of effective impulse control and emotional growth, subsequently, may be inhibited.

Research by Dean and Jacobson (1982) found that parents of learning problem children were generally defensive; they attempted to present a "good" image. The parents' tendency to internalize the feelings of self-blame and guilt only served to compound the difficulties already existing as a result of the child's situation.

With increasing maturity, the child naturally begins spending more time with peers. The parent may perceive this as rejecting behavior, especially since the child required a great deal of the family's energy and commitment in the past. A parent–child dependent/independent struggle can ensue. An enduring conflict and bitter feelings between the parent and child may be the unfortunate final outcome when a lack of parental understanding exists.

Single parents need to be aware that these aforementioned emotions are normal; indeed, they are common among all parents who have children with learning needs. Learning disability specialists (e.g., Kroncik, 1977) advise parents to deal effectively with these emotions and improve their emotional well-being by using positive action, manifested in the following ways:

- Plan for free-time. The use of outside resources keeps single parents from exhausting themselves physically or mentally.

- Interact with other single parents of children with learning needs. Single parents in support groups not only support each other emotionally, but also share information about available services.
- Take a realistic perspective and do not expect overnight miracles. It is unrealistic to expect immediate or totally satisfactory results.
- Be practical and flexible. If a plan or activity is ineffective, the parent should examine other alternatives.
- Be persistent. If a parent has asked for information or special services that are not provided in a reasonable time, the parent should pursue the request; reminders to professional personnel are often necessary.

For some single parents, professional advice and assistance is not needed; however, sometimes the emotional hardships involved in single parenting a child who has a learning problem become too overwhelming and difficult to handle alone. The single parent may face many extraneous problems, including: (a) financial constraints (Margalit, 1982); (b) health problems; (c) isolation; (d) educational limitations; and (e) poor home organization/control (McWhirter, 1980). In single parent families where there are many children, it is difficult to give the special child all the attention and encouragement that he or she may need (McWhirter, 1980). Conflicts between the single parent who has custody and the child's other parent may interfere with the time and energy these children require (Neifert and Gayton, 1973). Further, doctors visits, unclear diagnoses, and sibling problems can interfere with normal family functioning resulting in frustration, especially aimed at the child with special learning needs (Roth and Weller, 1985). In these and other cases, family/parent counseling is recommended (Margalit, 1982; Roth and Weller, 1985; Silver, 1983).

It is important for single parents to participate in parent education/counseling programs that meet their unique needs. Parent placement in an inappropriate program may pose further frustration in the home situation. Parent counseling that is broad-based and comprehensive enough to meet the many needs and diverse values, attitudes, and characteristics of single parents is the most effective (McWhirter, 1980).

There are many types of parent counseling. Among the most prevalent types are: (a) individual parent counseling to define and cope with a specific child's problem; (b) family counseling in which the family is seen as a unit (in the case of the single parent this may mean other persons than those ordinarily considered part of the nuclear family) and all explore problems together; and (c) parent group consultation where several single parents are brought together for a number of sessions to generate and share new knowledge about family behavior and interactions.

Counseling can also be educational for single parents; it may teach them about learning problems in general, child management, and behavior modification training. Finally, some programs emphasize the use of helpful suggestions to aid the family with a particular problem (McWhirter, 1980; Roth and Weiler, 1985).

Home Interventions

There are many effective approaches that the single parent can use in the home to assist the child with learning problems and improve the social-emotional climate for all family members. According to Rosenberg (1979), four requirements need to be met by single parents and their families before any home interventions are implemented. To be truly effective and involved, single parents need:

(1) Commitment. Decision by family members to work for the attainment of a particular goal for the child.
(2) Resources. Emotional and physical resources are required if the family members are to be able to maintain themselves, and solve new problems as they arise.
(3) Consensus. Agreement among family members regarding the nature of their goals, allocation of responsibilities, and the coordination of their efforts.
(4) Boundary permeability. Families maintain control over their internal affairs in order to survive as a unit. They also remain open to the information and materials that are required for their survival.

The preceding family requirements have been found to be the major determinants of parent performance for successful interventions and child development. Home interventions are useful and practical ways of involving single parents with their child's education. These intervention activities encompass many areas and may involve other individuals or community members.

Infancy

Until recently, psychology neglected the infant's mind as though infants were passive, impotent, and incapable of learning (Pines,

1966; Lee, 1976). William James described the infant's world as a "blooming, buzzing mass of confusion." With the exception of Piaget's theory, the first major theories of child development were more concerned with physical, physiological, and emotional development than they were with the mind (Lefrancois, 1983).

Piaget (1972) observed infants and children; he classified his observations by the stages through which children progress. A revolutionary theory of infant's and child's development was introduced. The infant's first stage is termed the sensorimotor stage and, acccording to Piaget, transpires from the time of birth until the age of two years. During the sensorimotor stage, the child's intelligence is primarily derived from, and expressed in, the motoric modality; no language or reasoning is evident at this earliest stage.

Nonetheless, by the age of two years, according to Piaget's theory, the infant dramatically progresses from an egocentric, quasi-animalistic existence to a world of preoperational thought. There is a dawning of understanding of cause-and-effect relationships and an ever-increasing language repertoire (Lefrancois, 1983).

Piaget's theory continues to affect current cognitive research on infants. At the infant's age of three weeks, or even earlier, researchers are now able to detect the presence of developmental or physiological difficulties that, if untreated, may profoundly affect the infant's later learning (White, 1985). Motor language, response, reflex, and hearing screening devices (e.g., McCarthy Scales and Kaufman Assessment Battery) are currently administered nationwide to infants in pilot programs, such as the Missouri New Parents as Teachers Project. The early detection and remediation of developmental and physiological difficulties (White, 1985) is thereby possible.

Parents, however, are urged to participate in stimulating preventative, rather than remedial, programs in the home with their infants (ages zero to three). For single parents (including divorced or separated men and women, widows and widowers with children, unmarried mothers, adoptive parents, stepparents and foster parents), economic problems, role conflicts, role shifts, and feelings of isolation and loneliness are common (McWhirter, 1980). Moreover, upon discovery that the infant of a single parent manifests a learning deficiency, one or more of three initial parental reactions further compound the existing problem; (a) anger, (b) disappointment, and/or (c) guilt (Love, 1970). The more visible the learning handicap, the greater the challenge confronting the parent in accepting the child and dealing with ambivalent feelings. Facilitating the environment to remediate the infant's existing deficiencies and prevent future learning problems presents additional time and emotional demands upon the parent.

As the infant's first teacher, however, the role of the parent is paramount. When the parent realizes the importance of his/her role in the child's development and recognizes the fact that he/she can influence the child's healthy educational growth, appropriate interaction strategies are sought.

Strategies for the Single Parent

The following strategies (Durkin, 1982; Hawley, 1985; White, 1985) are recommended for parents of infants in the development of the child's self-awareness, motor skills, listening skills, and language development.

Self-Awareness and Environment

- Give the child an ice cube. Let the child feel its texture and coldness and watch as it melts and changes.
- Purchase a stainless steel mirror (minimize size, five to six inches).
- Fill a box with colorful, safe objects. The child plays with each object. Substitute new objects frequently.
- Provide a walker (four to seven months of age is the optimal time). Supervise the infant at all times, however.
- Place large pictures on the child's wall. Talk about them with the child.
- Construct a "stabile," a mobile that does not move, for the infant ages three through nine weeks.

Motor Development

- Play the spider game, spiraling your finger from a distance to the child's nose. The child's eyes will follow.
- Provide simple books made of cloth. Read them together; orally label the pictures.
- Allow the child to climb. (Monitor at all times.)
- Play music with different rhythms. "Dance" with child to the rhythm.
- Give the child funnels, cups, and squeeze bottles for water play in the bathtub.
- Let the child scribble with large crayons and paper.

Listening Skills

— Give the child a talking toy that imitates animal or other sounds.
— Fill lidded plastic containers with different objects. The child shakes each container to hear (e.g.) beans, rice, coins, and carrot pieces.
— Play a tapping game. The parent taps once or twice; the infant imitates. Later, reverse roles and the parent taps in response to the infant.
— Find different stations on the radio for the child. Observe reactions to the voices, music, and sound effects. Later, allow the child to turn the radio dial.
— Sing to the child. Whistling, humming, and other sound effects are good attention-sustainers.

Language Development

— Recite nursery rhymes while dressing or bathing the baby or while walking.
— Elaborate the child's sentences or phrases. For example, if the child says, "Gi-Gi home," the parent replies, "Yes, Grandma went home this morning."
— Use visual aids such as magazine pictures, books, toys, and photographs. Describe each item to the child.
— Read to the child regularly. Notice when the child begins to lose interest. At this time change your voice, use motions, or begin another story or a new activity.
— Take the child for walks. Talk about each new sight and event as you walk.

When single parents need to work outside the home, White and Meyerhoff (1984) recommend that the child be cared for by a competent, nurturing caregiver in the child's own home, whenever possible. Small groups or individual care is recommended. Whatever the family circumstances, the manifestation of three qualities of the parent or caregiver are essential (White and Meyerhoff, 1984).

First, they must communicate to the infant the feelings of being warmly, deeply, securely, and consistently loved. Clear and firm limits are established and enforced.

Second, they act as the child's personal consultant. The parent takes the time to observe the child, interact on a regular basis, and **enhance** the activity of interest to the child at any given moment.

Finally, the parents or primary caregivers provide new and stimulating learning experiences for the infant. The home becomes a safe and yet fascinating "learning center" in which the child becomes actively involved in exploring, discovering, and learning at his/her own pace. A lack of environmental stimulation is responsible for many early, and later, learning problems (White and Meyerhoff, 1984).

As the child begins to learn and grow, the parents' confidence and pride in the child frequently increase. The parent is encouraged, therefore, to continue responding to the child and to facilitate his/her emerging skills. Regular visits to the pediatrician and, when necessary, referral to medical specialists such as pediatric audiologists, ophthamologists, or neurologists will also enhance the physical well-being and later intellectual functioning of the infant who shows evidence of motor or processing deficiencies.

Childhood $3-12$

Of all the individuals who have learning disabilities, most attention is focused on school-age children between the ages of five and eighteen (Barkley, 1981). It is during this time children are initially referred for learning problems and begin receiving remedial services to assist them in overcoming the learning need. Some predictions of learning disabilities, however, are apparent before five years of age (Trehub, 1977). Further, adolescents with learning needs are a new area in the field of learning disabilities (Lerner, 1981). This deserves its own discussion apart from problems of the primary-age child. Consequently, this section will focus on children between the ages of three and twelve.

According to Piaget's theory, children during this age period (three to twelve) progress from preoperational to concrete operational thinking. Preoperational children are able to manipulate objects and use representational skills, but they cannot produce accurate explanations for what they have done. Further, they focus only on a single attribute rather than on multiple attributes (Meyer and Dusek, 1979). When they reach the operational stage, children's actions are internalizable, reversible, and coordinated into systems that have laws that apply to the entire systems, not simply to the single operation itself.

These stages are sequential and the transition from one level to the next involves maturation. What is sometimes diagnosed as a learning problem in a child may be merely a lag in the maturation of certain processes (Lerner, 1981). For this reason, many children have only temporary learning problems. In other children, however, learning problems are not maturational and will remain with the individual through adulthood (Lerner, 1981). In both cases, the child exhibiting learning problems requires immediate and appropriate interventions to overcome the learning need.

For single parents, providing these interventions is often a difficult task due to the many personal and economic constraints in their lives. Notwithstanding, home interventions are an excellent means by which the parent can aid the child with learning needs academically, socially, and emotionally, thereby improving the emotional climate for all family members. Three of the more important interventions include: (a) limit-setting, (b) chores, and (c) play.

1. Limits

Children with learning needs are similar to normal children in: (a) their need to test limits, (b) their tendency to try to find the easiest way out of a situation, and (c) their attempts to "get the better" of an adult (Cruickshank, 1977). Children with learning problems, as well as normal children, need to know what is expected of them. Further, consistency is an important factor in discipline. When the single parent establishes appropriate limitations for the child, the child is offered the opportunity for unconditional acceptance, despite his/her sometimes undesirable behavior. Children with learning problems need regular and predictable patterns. As routine lessens, confusion tends to develop. It is important, therefore, to maintain a regular daily schedule for meals, play, homework, television, and bedtime. Changes in routine need to be explained in advance so the child is able to prepare him-/herself to carry out the changes.

2. Chores

Children with learning problems benefit from helping around the house with regular chores (Silver, 1983). Excusing the child from chores imparts the message that the child is inadequate, especially if siblings are required to do the work. Selecting tasks that maximize the possibility of the child's success, using knowledge of the child's strengths and weaknesses, is desirable. Clearly defined household chores and support assistance may be necessary before the child feels able to successfully complete the task alone. Accompany each part of the task with appropriate verbalization and definitions of related vocabulary words. Demonstrate clearly and model what is expected of the child. Provide support and assistance when the child works toward independence in performing the task. Merely telling the child what to do does not typically result in successful performance of the task. The child needs to know whatever sequential steps are necessary.

timer helps

Timelines for completion of tasks need to be clearly specified and enforced. The child needs to know and understand when the chore is to be initiated and completed in the form of an implicit contractual agreement. Successful completion is always rewarded. Approval is offered during the task, as well as immediately following full completion of the task. As progress occurs, the child's family responsibilities can increase. Parental demands that are reasonable and in line with those of the other children are realistic for use with learning-needs children. Responsibilities and demands are recognized not as punitive activities, but, rather, as part of normal family living.

3. Play

Play is one of the most effective means by which the child learns academic and social skills such as language, imagination, expression, and cooperation (Sutton-Smith, 1985). Moreover, the child and parent interact in a mutually pleasurable way. The child at play provides an outstanding opportunity for the parent to observe, whether as participant or spectator, the differential skills, interests, and needs of the child.

Single parents benefit from information concerning the purchasing of toys, games, and books. Items that may not be appropriate for children with learning problems include those that are overly complicated, considering the child's coordination and motor abilities. The child's functional age and developmental skills are important considerations when selecting toys for the child. Incorrect toy selections may result in the child's frustration. Adult participation, on an equal level, in the child's activities cannot be overemphasized.

Children cannot sustain attention in a solitary activity for any length of time. Interactive play provides an opportunity for the parent to share time and to communicate with the child. Consistency in scheduling play periods provides necessary structure in the child's day. Play with parent and peers is essential to the child's development; however, independent play frees the child from the distractions of other children and is also recommended (Cruickshank, 1977).

The child with learning problems will probably not be able to perform as well as other children of the same age on problem solving or coordination tasks. If several children are attracted to the activity, competition may develop, and the child who is unsuccessful and frustrated will probably lose interest and withdraw from the play. When the child is playing, numbers of toys might be kept to a minimum to avoid the child's becoming overwhelmed or overly excited. Specific games and activities that may facilitate growth in different areas of weakness for the child are listed in Appendix B at the conclusion of this chapter.

Strategies for the Parent

Additional strategies for single parents of children with learning needs include:

- Notify other family members of the child's learning needs. They may be able to communicate with the child more easily, thereby fostering a feeling of belonging, offering friendship, and providing support.
- Encourage the child to respond in complete sentences and not just phrases or one-word answers.
- Discuss items and concepts in the home with the child. For example, kitchen utensils and cooking equipment can be identified, discussed, and used by the child in ways appropriate to his/her level of maturity.
- Ask the child for only one thing at a time. Make simple demands and give simple instructions. Explain "why" if necessary.
- Allow the child to accomplish learned tasks without assistance.
- Set reasonable, challenging goals and do not make situations too easy.
- Limit the child's television time in order to increase his/her time at active learning tasks including reading, playing, or exploring.
- Establish eye contact before speaking; call the child's name and wait for acknowledgment with children who have figure-ground problems (i.e., difficulty selecting the sounds upon which to focus).
- Help the child to organize activities when he or she experiences a sequencing problem. For example, single parents can model what they want the child to do or place materials in the sequence in which they want the child to do things (Cruickshank, 1977; Daniels, 1982; McWhirter, 1980; Townes, Trupin, and Doan, 1979).

Sibling Issues

Single parents often need to spend more time with the child with learning problems than with their other children. They may, consequently, begin to feel guilty for slighting the others (Cruickshank, 1977). The best plans to provide equitable amounts of time to each child often fail because of unexpected situations occurring in the normal course of daily activities for the child with learning problems. Because of the absence of shared responsibilities (often present in "traditional" families), single parents may have less time to devote to each of the children than two parent families have. The problem child may become the focal point of family functioning (e.g., meals, family outings).

The tendency for the child with learning needs to require special attention is almost unavoidable. Single parents and their other children learn to accept this phenomenon as part of reality. Guilt can overwhelm the parent who does not realize that it is acceptable to give more attention to the child with learning problems than to the other children. A great deal of unnecessary emotional energy may be expended as the parent feels remorse for neglecting siblings; the normal relationships of the whole family may, as a result, be disrupted.

Providing each child with sufficient attention can be attained by careful scheduling and advance planning. Time can be devoted to other siblings when the child with learning problems is not present. Siblings need to know that they, too, can expect consistent, quality time alone with the parent; however, it is undesirable to set unusually or unreasonably high expectations for siblings in order to compensate for the child with learning needs (Vigilante, 1983). This situation, obviously, is detrimental and needs to be avoided.

Adolescent Interventions   13-18

Adolescents, ages thirteen to eighteen, form their own sub-group of individuals with learning needs. Specific problems related to this age are commonly recognized. Adolescents are ready to assume increasingly more responsibilities in the home. They are also beginning to participate in such "adult" tasks as career choices, dating, and driving and, similar to normal children, require assistance in dealing with these developmental tasks. Adolescents with learning problems, however, experience more difficulty in the transitional period between childhood and adulthood and need more assistance than do normal adolescents.

Strategies for the Parent

Interventions specific to the adolescent period for which the single parent can provide assistance (Houck, 1982; Silver, 1983) include: (a) household planning, (b) managing money, (c) purchasing clothing, (d) self-advocacy, (e) taking a driving test, (f) peer group activities, and (g) choosing a career. These issues are as relevant for the adolescent with learning problems as they are for normal adolescents.

Involvement in household activities such as planning a meal or trip provides opportunity for the adolescent to develop skills in planning ahead, seeking alternatives, and achieving a goal. The adolescent can be taught about household money management through the use of credit cards, savings accounts, and planning for future purchases.

Adolescents can be allowed to make decisions about clothing purchases while they learn about size and fabric differences, dry cleaning items, and clothing costs. By selecting appropriate clothing and items needed on trips (e.g., camping, vacations, over-nights), older children and young adults with learning problems learn to differentiate essential from nonessential items.

As adolescents mature toward young adulthood, they must begin to accept some, and later, most of the advocacy roles of adults. They may need help in learning to speak independently and clearly about their own needs.

Passing driving tests can be a problem for those individuals with difficulties in auditory perception and short-term memory. Requesting written directions from others and memorizing the route in advance can prove helpful for adolescents with learning needs.

Socially, adolescents with learning problems may have problems interacting with peers. For those individuals who have difficulty with reading, even a trip to a restaurant with friends may pose a major problem. One method of lessening social embarrassment involves the adolescent's waiting until last to order, and then choosing from what others have ordered (Silver, 1983). Additionally, copies of menus from local fast-food restaurants can be obtained prior to, or during, a restaurant visit so that the adolescent can practice reading them at home.

Choosing a career may represent a major problem for the student with learning problems. The specific abilities involved in different careers require realistic and careful consideration. Unfortunately, adolescents with learning needs often have trouble defining their strengths. Consequently, they may pursue occupations based on an underestimate of their abilities. Single parents can help the adolescent focus on his areas of strength. For those students who plan working for a college degree, there are technical schools and colleges offering special tutoring and resources for those with learning problems. Special program opportunities might be explored before the adolescent applies to a regular four-year college.

Tests may need to be modified for the learning disabled adolescent. For example, the Scholastic Aptitude Test can be taken untimed or with a preceptor who will read questions and record the answers (e.g., for dyslexics). Provided the indicators are favorable, adolescents with learning needs should be informed that they have reasonable probability of academic success if they are motivated, but that it may be more difficult and time-consuming for them than for the average student (Silver, 1983).

Social Interventions

Frequently, children with learning needs exhibit problems in social relationships. Compared with normal children, children with learning problems, as well as those from "broken homes," manifest higher rates of depression (Stevenson and Romney, 1984); behavioral/emotional problems (Epstein, Cullinan, and Nieminen, 1984); anxiety and lower self-esteem (Margalit and Zak, 1984); and deficient ability to interpret people and the environment (Weiss, 1984). Single parent strategies (Cruickshank, 1977) for facilitation of the child's socio-emotional development include:

— Be an interpreter for the child with learning needs to other parents (especially parents of children with whom the child plays), school personnel, athletic coordinators, scouting leaders, other club or team leaders, and neighbors. The parent of the child with learning needs may wish to inform these significant others in the child's life about his/her unique strengths and weaknesses to ensure that appropriate activities are developed.
— Be aware of the point at which the child begins to interfere with the play of others. The child may need to be withdrawn at this time and have his/her energies diverted temporarily. The child is more likely to be welcomed back by the children if they know his/her inappropriate behavior will not be allowed.
— Ascertain the amount of stimuli and kinds of situations the child can tolerate. Anticipation of new experiences will often distract a learning-needs child for many days in advance of the event, as well as for a period of time afterwards (e.g., parties, holidays, and vacations).
— Encourage the child to have outside peer interests (e.g., scouting, sports, music, art, etc.). The child with learning problems needs to become independent, and specific activities at which the child can excel will help him/her conceptualize independent functioning and success.

— Provide role models of the same sex as the absent parent for
children who live with only one parent. Big Brother/Sister programs, YMCA, YWCA, Boy and Girl Scouts, and the like provide
positive role-modelling opportunities. Additionally, involvement
in these organizations may help to ease the child's emotional and
self-concept problems, often experienced as a result of the scarcity
of available interaction time between the single working parent
and the child.

Psychological Interventions

Children with learning problems require a great deal of
understanding and support from adults, especially their parents.
Encouragement and acceptance from the parent is essential in providing the child with strong feelings of self-worth, competence, and
initiative. "The most important element in a child's eventual appreciation of his existence is the harmony of thought and action that
results from promoting strengths rather than deficits" (Mangold,
1980).

Single parents can do much to help the child with learning needs
develop a healthy self-concept. Specific interventions by the single
parent designed to impact a child's psychological well-being (Love,
1970; Yawkey, 1980) include:

— Learn from the child. The parent who listens and observes carefully uncovers clues about how the child approaches problems and
where the child's strengths and difficulties are located.
— Give extra reassurance. Praise and encouragement promote a
sense of accomplishment.
— Maintain the child's self-esteem and pride. Use constructive suggestions and positive reinforcement rather than negative statements or criticisms.
— Reward successes to develop confidence and a positive self-image.
— Encourage interests in children. Trips based on specific goals are
more beneficial than generalized sight-seeing excursions. For example, visiting the zoo to see the snakes is preferable to simply
visiting the zoo. Specific planned activities provide the framework
for directed, purposeful behavior and not generalized random
movement.
— Accept the child's own progress and areas of strength. Avoid com-
paring the child to others. It is important to recognize and frequently praise the child's accomplishments.
— Allow the child to do as much as he or she is able—physically,

socially, and academically. Too much parental overprotectiveness can lead to peer problems, discipline problems, and further school problems for the child.
— Let the child know it is acceptable to make mistakes and that mistakes are a part of the learning process.
— Seek counseling for the child if school failing results in anxiety, frustration, or other emotional problems (Margalit, 1982).

As the child begins to realize that the parent accepts him, his feelings of security increase. For children who have recently experienced a family divorce, feelings of guilt and self-blame are common. Compounding his anxieties may be the pressure to overcome learning problems and the fear of failure (Margalit, 1982). The parent's role, therefore, is crucial in insuring the child's feelings of self-worth, security, and well-being.

School Interventions

Results of recent research (McWhirter, 1980; Silver, 1983; Townes, Trupin, and Doan, 1979) indicate that the progress of children with learning needs is facilitated in all areas when the home environment supports and extends school programming. Single parents are instrumental in supplementing formal schooling by teaching children with learning needs many of the basic academic, social, self-help, communication, and vocational skills. Parents are viewed as educators in four ways (McWhirter, 1980): (a) they provide resources for learning; (b) they teach children in the home; (c) they manage their children's education through such activities as monitoring homework and coordinating the efforts of tutors and other agents; and (d) they function as socializers by learning and practicing recommended child-rearing techniques. A positive family influence is critical to the child's success in the classroom, in skill acquisition, in learning desirable behaviors, and in positive attitudes and motivation toward learning. The single parent, working alone, may require assistance in performing the task of "educator" successfully.

School Readiness

Preparing the child for school is a major challenge for the single parent of a preschooler who manifests early learning problems. An important contribution of the single parent is instilling in the child an interest in words, books, and reading (Durkin, 1982).

Leaving the teaching of reading solely to the teacher is neither an educationally nor psychologically sound practice. Parental involvement in reading readiness optimally begins before the child's entrance to school and continues throughout the school years (Vukelich, 1984). Durkin (1982) and Vukelich (1984) recommend several different activities and modelling behaviors for the parent in order to facilitate the child's word recognition and comprehension.

- Read to the child on a regular basis.
- Be a good literate model through reading and writing.
- Provide books, magazines, and other interesting materials for the child to read.
- Build a reading atmosphere at home. Establish a "library area" of age-appropriate and stimulating materials, for example.
- Talk and listen to the child.
- Exemplify a positive attitude toward reading, including rewarding and praising the child for reading.
- Provide experiences for the child that are reading-related (e.g. library trips) or experiences that can be used to stimulate interest in reading (e.g., a trip to the circus or local dairy).
- Read environmental signs and capture other reading opportunities in the environment, such as recipes, magazines, road maps, and so forth.
- Provide contact with paper and pencil.
- Write with the child. Encourage the child to write to a pen pal, a grandparent, or a favorite television star of his or her choice.
- Together, write lists of favorite words, such as foods, colors, or animals. Play creative games using the word lists; use the words in sentences and read them aloud.
- Point to similarities and differences among objects in the environment.
- Actively investigate the child's special talents and interests; provide books and other media by which the child can pursue the interest.

Symptoms

In school, children with learning problems often exhibit symptoms such as problems in reading, copying letters, and performing basic arithmetic. Specific symptoms of children's learning disabilities have been enumerated (Barkley, 1981; Bryan and Bryan, 1978; Daniels, 1983; Lerner, 1981): (a) behavioral problems, (b) reading deficits, (c) writing difficulties, and (d) arithmetic problems.

Specific behaviors exhibited by children in school that may indicate a learning problem include:

- Behavioral problems (for example, nervousness, impulsivity, anger, and frustration)
- Inability to adjust to new situations or tasks
- Difficulty in dealing with time factors
- Inability to see beyond the whole to the parts
- Lack of flexibility in responding to new situations
- Problems following directions
- Problems categorizing ideas or things
- Poor advance planning
- Perseveration
- Defeatist attitude toward school work
- Focus only on isolated events; failure to recognize how events are related
- Consistently late arrival to class
- Failure to bring home correct study material and/or ineffective study habits

Those children who have reading problems often exhibit the following behaviors (Lerner, 1981):

- Difficulty reproducing the sounds accurately
- Confusion with words and letters (may see them backwards)
- Difficulty building words from letters
- Inability to copy a visual image
- Inability to draw or copy shapes
- Difficulty in drawing conclusions due to reasoning deficiencies
- Failure to demonstrate language growth and vocabulary acquisition
- Problems remembering and repeating sentences
- Slow rate of reading
- Poor comprehension

Additionally, the child may experience difficulty in writing. Frequently, children who encounter reading problems also manifest weaker writing skills. Most learning problems are language-based and are manifested through the related areas of reading and writing (Durkin, 1982). Six writing behaviors may warn the parent of a child's weakness in this area:

- Writing from right to left
- Mirror writing
- Poor writing quality

- Trouble transferring information from the blackboard or workbook to the paper
- Disorganized note-taking
- Incomplete assignments

Children with visual perceptual problems often have difficulty performing basic math. These children may or may not concurrently exhibit reading or writing deficits. Children who have mathematics learning needs may exhibit the following behaviors:

- Inability to use and understand number concepts
- Reversal of the order of figures
- Failure to understand order involved in counting
- Problems remembering and repeating numbers

School Facilitation Strategies

The child with learning problems requires assistance both at home and school to learn metacognitions and strategies to overcome these problems. Single parents who are actively involved in all aspects of the child's development and education are able to exert a very positive influence upon the child's academic progress. School-related techniques for single parents include the following:

- Listen to the child when she talks about school. Support her when she has had a trying day. Shifting the blame, however, to the teacher is to be avoided. The parent helps the child understand that learning is important to life and is the responsibility of the learner as well as the teacher.
- Improve communication by determining whether the child prefers information received auditorially or visually. Learning if the child more easily remembers information from books (visual) or anecdotes and discussions (auditory) can aid in identifying the child's primary modality for learning (McWhirter, 1980).
- Provide a tutor for the child to bridge gaps that may have occurred between skills when the child's learning problems interfered with the acquisition and/or retention of academic material.
- Help reinforce what the child has learned at school through special summer activities (for example, trips to museums or geographical sites discussed in science or social studies).
- Provide a special, prominent place for the child's school work; refrigerators or bulletin boards are popular display areas.
- Observe the child's education directly by volunteering as adjunct teacher in the classroom, field trip chaperone, or in other school activities.

For those children who receive special education services due to severe learning problems, single parents need to become even more involved with schooling (Schulz, 1982). Recommended techniques include the following:

- Exercise rights based on P.L. 94-142, including taking an active role in the decision-making process and, when necessary, appealing any decision related to evaluation, placement, and educational approach.
- Learn as much as possible about the child's problems and about the evaluation and treatment of learning handicapped children, in general. Read about the subject and talk with teachers and other professionals, such as doctors, and with parents whose children have similar problems.
- Keep in touch with the child's teachers and others in the school district who are responsible for the child's education, and schedule appointments at convenient times to discuss the child's education.
- Contact the individual who can help solve a problem or answer needed questions when they occur. In any contact with professionals or other persons, remain objective and present concerns to which others can respond constructively.
- Keep a notebook about the child's education and retain all copies of reports, educational plans, and communications to and from school officials. Request that all communications be in written form. If a conference took place by telephone, a letter is requested to confirm decisions; thus, the records remain complete.
- Keep dated notes on private observations of the child. Anecdotal records are the parent's own documentation and provide a baseline against which the child's improvement in a given ability is determined.
- Ask for progress reports on a regular basis and store each, sequentially, in a notebook (Heward, Dardig, and Rosett, 1979; Kronick, 1977; Loftus and Walter, 1981; Schulz, 1982).

Homework

Assistance with homework is one of the most relevant and important intervention approaches by single parents working with a child who manifests learning problems (Silver, 1983). The parent can learn how best to approach homework with the child based upon the child's special needs. He does not tell the child how to do the homework or complete it for her. If homework difficulty occurs, a conference with the school staff is scheduled to discuss the difficulties and develop a strategy for helping the child. Suggestions for homework and school preparation proposed by Silver (1983) to assist single parents include:

Homework

(1) Help the child organize school materials. A system, implemented with assistance from the teacher, may be required.

(2) Help the child overcome routine difficulties such as trouble opening lockers. The parent might have the child, in this case, carry all supplies in a large gym bag or backpack.

(3) Be certain that homework instructions are understood. Memory problems, poor handwriting, or distractibility cause children to copy incomplete or incorrect assignments. Have the teacher check the child's assignment pad for accuracy or give the student a written copy of what is expected.

(4) Monitor the load of homework. A teacher may expect a given task to require fifteen minutes. The child, however, may require one hour's time because of slow reading or handwriting. Schedule a meeting with the teacher to discuss the appropriate amount of homework.

(5) Help promote concentration by providing the child with a private, uncluttered area with few distractions and little noise in which to do homework. Keep only the book and paper on the desk. Try, also, to use simple, solid colors and ascertain that minimal visual distractions appear in the room.

(6) Help plan work time by structuring a specific time each day or on weekends for doing work.

(7) Help prepare in advance by getting the child ready for the next school day. Be certain that all books, papers, special clothing, lunch money, and other materials are ready in the morning to alleviate confusion.

(8) Schedule a conference, with the child in attendance, to devise a plan for implementation in the event of unsubmitted homework. One strategy discussed at the conference could involve the teacher's sending home a list of the homework requirements each day. A second strategy involves handling the problem directly by denying the child certain privileges (for example, recess; during this time the child completes the unfinished homework assignments).

Adolescence

Hopefully, by the time a learning needs child reaches adolescence, he has acquired sufficient behavioral and learning strategies to function adequately in the secondary classroom. Some problems manifested by adolescents with learning needs, however, may require further interventions. Adolescents who rebel against special education and wish to remain in regular classes may be able to have their supportive help transferred to an out-of-school, nonpublic time.

Those students who have, in the past, accepted medication may now refuse to do so. Adolescents with special needs may be embarrassed about being singled out among peers. Instead of insisting that the adolescent visit the school nurse, the teacher might arrange for the school nurse to administer his medication in a more private area of the school.

In elementary school, the regular or special education teacher manages the child's day. She monitors class assignments and even the child's social groups. In contrast, the secondary student with learning problems now assumes major responsibility for organizing new information (e.g., listening and taking notes), as well as the entire school day (e.g., finding classrooms, learning names of classmates and teachers).

Adolescents require an even greater degree of assistance, through parents and teachers, in learning organizational skills. An orientation, prior to admittance, delineating the expected behaviors of a student in that particular secondary school is helpful. The orientation might include: (a) a tour of the school's facilities and student's classrooms; (b) assistance to the student as he or she memorizes teachers' names, classes, and lunch times; and (c) an opportunity for the student to meet the special education teacher (Houck, 1982; Silver, 1983).

Professional Involvement

Single parents of children with learning problems are often ill-informed about the implications of learning problems (Dembinski and Mauser, 1977). Trying to comprehend the legal issues, special programs, evaluation process, and so forth involved with a learning-needs child is frequently quite overwhelming for a parent. The parent needs assistance, especially initially, in learning how to deal with a child who has learning problems.

Working with the Single Parent

School professionals, such as guidance counselors, nurses, teachers, and administrators, who work with children who manifest learning needs can do a great deal to enhance the effectiveness and ease the strain often experienced by single parents. Professional approaches suggested by Dembinski and Mauser (1977) include:

- Use terminology the parent can understand. Simple English is the best means of communication. Avoid the use of technical terms unless they are fully explained.
- Use tear-off sheets with school requests for meetings; in this way, the parent is able to respond easily and immediately.
- If the school budget permits, use a self-addressed envelope.
- Personalize invitations to meetings either through written notes or telephone calls.
- Help the parent understand the system. Provide written and verbal explanations of school policies and procedures.
- Encourage the parent to ask questions.
- Send information home before meetings so that parents are able to familiarize themselves with the information and prepare for the meeting.
- Give parents materials to read about effective teaching strategies that parents can implement in the home.
- Give parents copies of all reports.
- Inform the parent in advance of possible problems his or her child may encounter with peers, sports, academics, and other areas.
- Be readily available to the single parent to provide needed assistance, answer questions, or talk about a particular problem manifested by the child with learning needs.

Conclusion

As divorce continues its upward trend and more parents become single parents, the percentage of single parent families with children who have learning needs will also rise (Lefrancois, 1983). These special families require a great deal of assistance to facilitate normal family functioning.

In the home, parents who are committed to remediating the child's learning needs must: (a) develop emotional and physical resources; (b) reach familial consensus; and (c) learn to survive as a unit while, at the same time, share responsibilities with the community. Infants, children, and adolescents alike require the parent's active awareness of, and involvement in, their developmental processes. Through early detection of problems, appropriate use of remediation strategies, close and regular school involvement, and contact with referral agencies when necessary, the parent helps to ensure the child's optimal development.

As is noted in Figure 6.1, positive parent behaviors facilitate the child's maximal emotional and learning behavior. As parents solicit effective assistance from outside resources, a sense of equilibrium is established; feelings of isolation tend to diminish. Resultingly, the parent begins to accept and interact more positively with the child. The child's feeling of security is strengthened, thus increasing his/her likelihood of improved emotional and academic performance. The ultimate result is an enhanced parent–child relationship.

Appendix A

Assessment Techniques for Detecting Learning Problems

			AGES		
Assessment Techniques	2–5	6–9	10–13	14–16	17+
Cognitive/General Intelligence					
Kaufman Assessment Battery for Children	X	X	X		
McCarthy Scales of Children's Abilities	X	X			
Stanford-Binet	X	X	X	X	X
Wechsler Intelligence Scale for Children–Revised		X	X	X	
Wechsler Preschool and Primary Scale of Intelligence	X	X			
Educational/Academic Achievement					
Detroit Test of Learning Aptitude	X	X	X	X	X
Key Math Arithmetic Test		X	X		
Metropolitan Achievement Test		X	X	X	X
Peabody Individual Achievement		X	X	X	X
Peabody Picture Vocabulary Test	X	X	X	X	X
Wide Range Achievement Test	X	X	X	X	X
Woodcock-Johnson Psycho-Educational Battery	X	X	X	X	X
Woodcock Reading Mastery Test		X	X	X	X
Visual-Motor Tests					
Bender Gestalt Test for Young Children	X	X	X		

Developmental Test of Visual-Motor Integration	X	X	X	X	
Developmental Test of Visual Perception	X	X	X		
Projective/Emotional Tests					
Human Figure Drawing	X	X	X	X	X
Kinetic Family Drawing	X	X	X	X	X
Rorschach Inkblot Test	X	X	X	X	X
Rotter Incomplete Sentences	X	X	X	X	X

Appendix B

Play Activities for Specific Learning Deficits

Gross-Motor Activities

Backyard equipment or neighborhood playgrounds or parks
Climbing apparatus and jungle gym
Swings
Swimming
Team sports for older children (basketball, baseball, soccer, etc.)

Eye–Hand Coordination Problems

Darts
Pogo sticks
Target activities
Bicycles
Scooters
Checkers
Card games
Toys with large pieces

Memory

Concentration
Simon Says
Personalized memory games about previous situations, past
  holidays, meals, stories, etc.

Visual

Dot to dot pictures
Mazes
Spelling with alphabet cereal

Creating a scrapbook with a common theme or elements using pictures or words

Paint by numbers

Cut up comic strips and have the child arrange them into the proper sequence

Visual-Motor

Pick-up sticks
Jumping rope
Ball and jacks
Marbles
Hopscotch
Games of catch and throwing
Yo-Yo
Ping-pong
Table pool
Etch-A-Sketch
Beads
Checkers
Crossword puzzles
Lacing cards
Scrabble
Puzzles
Tinker toys
Spill and Spell
Copying visual designs and symbols
Drawing pictures by analyzing and drawing the component parts in sequence

Arithmetic

Bingo
Battleship
Chinese Checkers
Chutes and Ladders
Concentration
Dominoes
Flash cards
Pay Day
Uno cards

Auditory

Games that require a response to sound (e.g., Simon Says and musical chairs)
Rhyming games

Child identifies sounds while eyes are closed
Sentences, poems, recipes, etc., that the child can repeat
Remembered events during the day that the child can share
Simple poems or jokes the child can remember
Tongue twisters
Walkie-Talkie
Radio
Tape recorder
Talking books

Fine-Motor/Perceptual Problems

Sort household items (e.g., silverware, buttons, socks, nuts, bolts)
String beads
Sew and cut
Open and close things
Differentiate between various shapes, colors, and materials
Scraping carrots, potatoes
Sharpening pencils
Washing hands with a rotating motion
Using a manual can or bottle opener

To Stimulate Reasoning and Real-Life Situations

Crosswords
Password
Family Fued
Finger puppets
Game of the states
Go to the head of the class
Match me
Parchesi
Pay day
Scrabble
Sorry
Monopoly
Think of a word
Ungame
Twenty questions
Tic-tack dough
Mastermind
Clue

(Adapted from McWhirter, 1980 and *A home intervention handbook;*
The Mississippi State Department of Education, 1983.)

References

BARKLEY, R. "Learning Disabilities," in *Behavioral Assessment of Childhood Disorders,* E. J. Mash and L. G. Terdal, eds., New York:Guilford Press (1981).

BARTOLOME, P. "The Changing Family and Early Childhood Education," in *Changing Family Lifestyles: Their Effect on Children,* L. Martin, ed., Washington, D.C.:Association for Childhood Education International, pp. 9–13 (1982).

BRONFENBRENNER, U. *The Ecology of Human Development,* Cambridge, MA:Harvard University Press (1979).

BRONFENBRENNER, U. "The Challenge of Social Change to Public Policy and Developmental Research," presented at the annual meeting of the Society for Research in Child Development (1974).

BRYAN, T. and J. Bryan. *Understanding Learning Disabilities.* Sherman Oaks, CA: Alfred Publishing Co. (1978).

CRUICKSHANK, W. *Learning Disabilities in Home, School and Community.* Syracuse, NY:Syracuse University Press (1977).

DANIELS, P. *Teaching the Gifted/Learning Disabled Child.* Rockville, MD:Aspen Publications (1983).

DANIELS, S. "From Parent-Advocacy to Self-Advocacy. A Problem of Transition," *Exceptional Education Quarterly,* 3:17–24 (1982).

DEAN, R. and B. Jacobson. "MMPI Characteristics for Parents of Emotionally Disturbed and Learning Disabled Children," *Journal of Consulting and Clinical Psychology,* 50:775–777 (1982).

DEMBINSKI, R. and A. Mauser. "What Parents of Learning Disabled Really Want from Professionals," *Journal of Learning Disabilities,* 10:578–584 (1977).

DURKIN, D. *Getting Reading Started.* Boston, MA:Allyn and Bacon (1982).

Education for All Handicapped Children Act, PL 94-142 (U.S.), November 29, 1975 (1982).

EPSTEIN, M., D. Cullinan, and G. Nieminen. "Social Problems of Learning Disabled and Normal Girls," *Journal of Learning Disabilities,* 17:609–611 (1984).

HAWLEY, B. S. "Working Toward Reading Readiness with a Two-Year-Old Child," unpublished manuscript, Kingston, RI:University of Rhode Island, Department of Education (1985).

HETHERINGTON, E., M. Cox, and R. Cox. "Effects of Divorce on Parents and Children," in *Nontraditional Families: Parenting and Child Development,* M. E. Lamb, ed., Hillsdale, NJ:Lawrence Erlbaum Associates, Inc. (1982).

HEWARD, W., J. Dardig, and A. Rosett. *Working with Parents of Handicapped Children.* Columbus, Ohio:Merrill, Inc. (1979).

HOUCK, C. *The Learning Disabled Adolescent: Parents and School Personnel Working Together–Looking Toward the Future.* Office of Special Education and Rehabilitative Services, ed., Washington, D.C. (1982).

KAUFMAN, A. S. and N. L. Kaufman. *The Kaufman Assessment Battery for Children (ABC),* Circle Pines, MN: American Guidance Service (1983).

KENNISTON, K. and the Carnegie Council on Children. *All Our Children.* New York:Harcourt Brace Jovanovich (1977).

KRONCIK, D. "Learning from Living," *Academic Therapy,* 13:225–232 (1977).

LEE, C. L. *Personality Development in Childhood.* Belmont, CA:Wadsworth (1976).

LEFRANCOIS, G. *Of Children.* Belmont, CA:Wadsworth (1983).

LEMASTERS, E. E. *Parents in Modern America.* Homewood, IL:The Dorsey Press (1974).

LERNER, J. *Learning Disabilities.* Boston:Houghton Mifflin Co. (1981).

LOFTUS, L. and V. Walter. *For Parents of Handicapped Children: Tips for Working with School Personnel.* Office of Special Education and Rehabilitative Services, Washington, D.C. (1981).

LOVE, H. *Parental Attitudes Toward Exceptional Children.* Springfield, IL:Charles C. Thomas (1970).

MANGOLD, S. S. "Nurturing High Self-Esteem in Visually Handicapped Children," in *The Self-Concept of the Young Child,* T. D. Yawkey, ed., Provo, Utah:The Brigham Young University Press, pp. 177–186 (1980).

MARGALIT, M. "Learning Disabled Children and Their Families: Strategies of Extension and Adaptation of Family Therapy," *Journal of Learning Disabilities,* 15:594–595 (1982).

MARGALIT, M. and I. Zak. "Anxiety and Self-Concept of Learning Disabled Children," *Journal of Learning Disabilities,* 17:537–539 (1984).

MCCARTHY, J. and J. McCarthy. *Learning Disabilities.* Boston, MA:Allyn and Bacon (1964).

MCWHIRTER, J. "Working with Parents of Learning Disabled Children," in *Parent Education and Intervention Handbook,* R. Abidin, ed., Springfield, IL:Charles C. Thomas (1980).

MEYER, W. and J. Dusek. *Child Psychology.* Lexington, MA:D.C. Heath and Company (1979).

NEIFERT, J. and W. Gayton. "Parents and the Home Program Approach in the Remediation of Learning Disabilities," *Journal of Learning Disabilities,* 2:85–89 (1973).

O'NEILL, W. *Divorce in the Progressive Era.* New Haven, CT:Yale University Press (1967).

PETERS, D. and C. Raupp. "Developing the Self Concept in the Exceptional Child," in *The Self-Concept of the Young Child,* T. D. Yawkey, ed., Provo, Utah:The Brigham Young University Press (1980).

PIAGET, J. "Intellectual Development from Adolescence to Adulthood," *Human Development,* 15:1–12 (1972).

PINES, M. *Revolution in Learning: The Years from Birth to Six.* New York:Harper & Row (1966).

ROSENBERG, S. *Family and Parent Variables Affecting Outcomes of a Parent Medicated Intervention.* ERIC Document no. 158471 (1979).

ROTH, L. and C. Weller. "Education/Counseling Models for Parents of Learning Disabled Children," *Academic Therapy,* 20:487–495 (1985).

SALHOLZ, E. "The Marriage Crunch," *Newsweek,* 107, 22:54–61 (June 2, 1986).

SCANZONI, J. *Shaping Tomorrow's Family, Vol. 43.* Beverly Hills:Sage Publications (1983).

SCHULZ, J. "A Parent Views Parent Participation," *Exceptional Education Quarterly,* 3:17–24 (1982).

SILVER, L. "Therapeutic Interventions with Learning Disabled Students and Their Families," *Topics in Learning and Learning Disabilities,* 3:48–58 (1983).

STEVENSON, D. and D. Romney. "Depression in Learning Disabled Children," *Journal of Learning Disabilities,* 17:579–582 (1984).

SUTTON-SMITH, B. "The Child at Play," *Psychology Today,* 19:64–65 (1985).

TOWNES, B., E. Trupi, and R. Doan. "Parent-Directed Remediation for Learning Disabled Children," *Academic Therapy,* 15:173–184 (1979).

TREHUB, S. "Infant Antecedents: A Search for the Precursors of Learning Disabilities," in *Topics in Child Neurology,* M. E. Blow, I. Papin, and M. Kinsbourne, eds., New York:Spectrum (1977).

United States Office of Education. "Assistance to States for Education of Handicapped Children: Procedures for Evaluating Specific Learning Disabilities," *Federal Register,* 42, pp. 65082–65085 (1977).

VIGILANTE, F. "Working with Families of Learning Disabled Children," *Child Welfare,* 62:429–436 (1983).

VUKELICH, C. "Parents' Role in the Reading Process: A Review of Practical Suggestions and Ways to Communicate with Parents," *The Reading Teacher,* 37:472–477 (1984).

WEISS, E. "Learning Disabled Children's Understanding of Social Interactions of Peers," *Journal of Learning Disabilities,* 17:612–615 (1984).

WHITE, B. L. *The First Three Years of Life.* Englewood Cliffs, NJ:Prentice-Hall (1985).

WHITE, B. L. and M. K. Meyerhoff. "What Is Best for the Baby?" in *The Infants We Care For,* L. L. Dittmann, ed., The National Association for the Education of Young Children (1984).

WHITFIELD, E. and K. Freeland. "Divorce and Children: What Teachers Can Do," in *Changing Family Lifestyles: Their Effect on Children,* L. Martin, ed., Washington, D.C.:Association for Childhood Education International, pp. 19–20 (1982).

ZINTL, R. T. and R. B. Thomas. "The Baby Boomers Turn Forty," *Time,* 127(20):22–41 (May, 1986).

CHAPTER 7

Language and Social Development of the Child from the Single Parent Family

SUSAN L. TROSTLE
FRANCIS J. DI VESTA

THE TRADITIONAL AMERICAN family—two parents, nuclear, nonworking mother—is no longer the typical American family (Belsky, Steinberg, and Walker, 1982). In fact, if one adheres to this definition of the traditional family, it is discovered that the majority of American families have partially or completely broken with the "traditional" image. Indeed, alternative lifestyles play a very prominent and ever-increasing influence in today's society. These lifestyles affect the characteristics of the social environment of the family with consequent implications for the child's cognitive, linguistic, social, and personality development.

The Changing American Family

Alternative or nontraditional lifestyles include communal living groups, single unmarried mothers, separated or divorced couples who share the custody of their children, and unmarried couples who reside together and rear one or more children (Lamb, 1982). Many of these alternative lifestyles were initiated during the counterculture movement that characterized the 1960s and have continued to affect significantly the familial social climate during the last two decades. For example, 45 percent of children born in the United States today will spend at least one year living with a single parent. The number of one-parent families has doubled during the past ten years (Umansky, 1983).

Many demographic differences exist between alternative and traditional (two parent) families. Mobility rates, maternal versus paternal employment patterns, and economic status are among the most obvious differences between the two living styles (Eiduson, Kornfein, Zimmerman, and Weisner, 1982). The studies of mobility rates show that during the child's first eighteen months of life, for example, 46 percent of the single parent families moved two or more times; only 19 percent of the two parent families moved more than once during the same period of time. With regard to employment patterns, the father is the main wage earner in traditional families during the child's first few years. The father typically works consistently and regularly in occupations that are rated highest on scales of vocational competency. The traditional family's income is, on the average, more than three times greater than that of the alternative family's income. The economic status of the traditional family, thus, is characterized by economic advantage, a more stable lifestyle, and a consistently improving financial status in contrast to the alternative or the single parent family (Lamb, 1982). The wider the degree of variation from the "traditional" family, then, the greater is the potential risk to the child in terms of economic advantage and lifestyle stability. These differences and the possible resultant effects upon the personal development of children in the respective families have been the source of growing interest and concern among children's advocates—parents, caregivers, teachers, and researchers.

The Working Mother

In families where both parents work, time constraints necessarily limit the number of joint activities in which family members can participate. Customarily, the woman is primarily responsible for the domestic chores and care of the children. With partial or no responsibility by the man, the ensuing overload and resultant pressures are experienced most acutely by the working mother. Provisions for child care services are often equally necessary in families where two parents work as well as in single parent families. The effects of maternal employment and single parenthood are often reflected in departures from the traditional family in: (a) the need for a substitute child care setting, (b) constrained maternal and paternal attitudes toward parenthood and employment, (c) the effects of the demands of employment, and (d) the results of limited sharing of familial responsibilities. This set of variables may incur negative effects on the child's language and social development.

Overall, the studies of the effects of maternal employment on child development tend to be inconclusive. Nevertheless, a consistent finding from the multitude of studies that have been conducted indicates that children of employed mothers have fewer sex-stereotyped values and expectations than do children of unemployed mothers (Lamb, 1982). There is substantial evidence, moreover, that daughters are more achievement-oriented when their mothers are employed than when they are not. The positive or negative effects of maternal employment upon the children may ultimately depend upon other, related variables such as parental attitude toward the employment, economic factors, and the availability of child care services.

The Need for Child Care Services

Regardless of the place in which child care transpires – the home or the school setting – the care providers themselves comprise the most important aspect of quality care (Belsky et al., 1982). Considering the fact that language is essential to the cognitive and social development of all children, caregivers face the awesome responsibility of providing environments conducive to frequent and high quality interactions for the children for whom they are responsible. The child's home and the day care center or school often contrast markedly in the types of experiences – social, emotional, academic, and physical – they provide for children.

Language patterns, regulatory strategies, physical environment, and value codes represent areas of potential inconsistencies between home and day care (Belsky et al., 1982). Continuity in the physical and social environment enhances the young child's development; for the older child this continuity may be less critical. These findings imply that, especially for younger children, it is essential to establish and maintain frequent communication between the parent and the caregiver in order to eliminate discrepancies in expectations (Belsky et al., 1982).

The child in the child care center experiences more interactions with peers – both positive and negative – than the child who is reared at home. Also, for children who attend day care, there is evidence of increased aggression toward peers and adults, less cooperation with adults and greater involvement in educational activities once they enter school. Other studies have linked preschool program enrollment to accelerated listening skills, paired associate learning, and perspective-taking competencies for the single parent child (Kadar-Sugar, 1980; Adams, 1982).

In summary, the evidence indicates that the effects of quality day care need not be deleterious and, indeed, may be very beneficial to the child from the single parent family. There exists an ever-increasing need for child care services in the United States today

(Belsky et al., 1982). The well-documented effects of day care enrollment upon children imply that caregivers need to provide consistently high quality services.

The Divorced Parent

The all too familiar, yet disturbing, fact is that one out of every two
marriages in the United States today will eventually end in divorce
(Lefrancois, 1983). Consequently, an examination of the personal
and social implications for each member of the broken family is
needed. "Families in which the parents had divorced encounter
many more stresses and difficulties in coping, which were reflected
in disturbances in personal and social adjustments and family relations, than did nondivorced families" (Hetherington, Cox, and Cox,
1982, p. 285). Many households headed by mothers are exposed to excessive stresses. As a result, they require additional support
systems. The ultimate outcomes of divorce upon the child are determined by factors such as age of the child, sex of the custodial parent,
socioeconomic status, culture, and ethnicity.

Recent studies illustrate the effects of divorce upon children's
receptive and expressive language capacities (Mofidi-Farkhondeh,
1981). Children from non-divorced families score consistently higher
on both receptive and expressive language tests than do children
from divorced families. The language scores of girls from traditional
families are significantly higher than the scores of girls from
divorced households. Moreover, children in families where incomes
were in the $12,000–$17,999 range scored significantly higher in
receptive and expressive language than children from families
where incomes were in the $0–$5,999 range (Mofidi-Farkhondeh,
1981). In general, when compared with more advantaged children
from intact families, children of divorce may confront more language, personal, and social adjustment problems.

Frequently, the circumstances of the divorce limit the amount of
time the estranged or separated parent is able to spend with the
child. During recent years the controversy concerning "quality time"
versus "quantity time" has been the subject of considerable discussion and investigation for parents and researchers. Amount of time
spent with the child is an insufficient consideration. The *quality* of
the time spent is equally important; stimulation, challenge, opportunity for expression and learning, and use of leisure time are all
means of increasing quality of time spent.

Quality time, by itself, may not provide the desirable parent–child
interaction found in quality *plus* quantity. In an insightful, candid

report concerning the effects of his own divorce reported in *Esquire* magazine, C. W. Smith (1985), alias "Uncle Dad," states:

> When we're being honest, we admit that quality time is that rare moment when a stretch of ordinary time is interrupted by an unexpected burst of genuine rapport. To say, "We will now have quality time," whether anybody feels like it or not, is like saying, "We will now have fun, or else." We fear this truth: that the necessary preparation for *quality* time is *quantity* time, and that we can't give [Smith, 1985, p. 75].

Divorced fathers and mothers are forced to recognize that there is simply no substitute for being there. When separation or divorce is imminent, Smith (1985) recommends: Whether or not she/he lives with the child, the perceptive divorced parent pays close attention to the language and social development of the child.

The possible combinations of the characteristics of the changing family form a multitude of complex social interaction patterns. The family composition [e.g., mother and child(ren) or father and child(ren)] may determine the nature of the behaviors available for the child to imitate and the opportunities for imitation. The absence or presence of one parent (for example, the father only) may affect the quality of the language environment for the infant and child. The following section addresses the infant's and the child's sequential language stages, each of which is critical to overall language development. Quality parental facilitation of each stage exerts strong influence upon a child's language development.

Development of Language

Developmental psychologists have only recently provided direct evidence of the remarkable capabilities for learning possessed by the young infant. This evidence dismisses the earlier conceptions of a completely aimless and vacuous organism passively waiting to be filled with world knowledge. Such conceptions were evident in Shakespeare's poetic view of an infant as "mewling and puking in his mother's arms" or John Locke's metaphor of the baby's mind as a "tabula rasa"—a blank slate to be written on—or William James' perception of the infant as a bewildered newcomer to a worldly environment, "so assailed by all sense organs and entrails simultaneously that the world could only be viewed as a blooming, buzzing confusion."

At the time when those authors attempted descriptions of the child's "mind," the means of studying infant attention, perceptions, cognitions, and capabilities were unavailable. They had to depend on subjective impressions or incomplete data. Today, laboratory techniques are available for making observations about how infants process information. For example, systematic observations of eye movements may indicate to what stimuli the infant attends. Increased sucking responses may indicate heightened motivation. The infant of a few months can be reinforced for simple responses (e.g., the sucking response) if the response "controls" movement of an external event (such as the turning of a clown by an experimenter). Empirical data gathered by these methods, in conjunction with the theories of developmental psychologists, social psychologists, and psycholinguists, indicate that the beginnings of social and language behaviors are manifested in the very early days of the infant's life, if not during the gestation period. For example, the imitative response can be observed at twelve days when the child will imitate a person sticking out his/her tongue, or, a little later, the child will blink back in imitation of the response in another person. At one month, the infant can detect the shape of the mouth and lip movements that correspond to different vowel sounds. Between six and eight months, the infant is able to distinguish sounds of its own language from other sounds. The evidence also suggests that the infant is able to produce most of the phonemes present in all languages, some of which may drop out by adulthood (e.g., Japanese infants can produce the "ell" phoneme that adult Japanese find hard to produce). A skilled linguist listening to a recording of the six- to eight-month-old baby's babbling can detect the language to which the baby has been exposed.

There are many universals—behaviors that are present in all humans. Included among them are capabilities for learning language and for imitating others. The direction and the quality of that development depends upon the kind of input the child receives from the environment and how responsive the environment (parents, etc.) is to the infant's responses. There are many remarkable achievements by the infant that are the beginnings of the young child's cognitive progress in spatial, conceptual, and number skills (Sophian, 1984). Some of these will be discussed in more detail, within the context of the single parent family, in the sections that follow.

General Characteristics of Language Development

A general description of the characteristics of language and speech development are shown in Table 7.1. It is based on Menyuk's (1971) summary of a number of observations based on research. The reader should note that the chronology is approximate and should not be construed as normative.

Table 7.1. The sequence of emerging language behaviors.

Birth to 6 months	*The infant period.* The child produces such sounds as grunts, cries, gasps, shrieks, chuckling, and cooing (at four months).
6 months to 9 months	*The babbling period.* The child produces units of utterances called babbling that differ from one situation to another. These units begin to be acoustically similar to adult utterances because the child sloughs off the irrelevant phonemes rather than acquiring new phonemes.
9 months	*The jargon period.* Stresses and intonation patterns in strings of utterance units clearly correspond to those of the adult. Some imitation of general language-like patterns can be identified. Specific morphemes cannot be distinguished easily by the listener.
9 months to 1 year	*The quiet period.* The decrease in vocalization during this period of development is interesting. Language habits continue to develop but changes are not immediately apparent to the observer. One reason for this period of relative quiet may be the discontinuity in language development between the previous stage and next stages; a transition occurs from the use of jargon to the use of words as the adult knows them.
1 year to 2 years	*The holophrastic stage.* The child uses single words to indicate whole phrases. He can use basic structure, but transformational rules to produce the surface structure have not been acquired. The single word is the start of the child's vocabulary. Preconventional "words" are considered words by the parent because a given sound pattern is used consistently is similar situations (for example, using "muk" for milk). These vocalizations sound like words and may be considered words by the prideful parents.
	The child understands much of what he is told. He demonstrates his comprehension by responding in a way that is meaningful to the adult—he may obey a command or point to an object.
	At the end of this period, the child produces from twenty words (at about eighteen months) to 200 words (at about twenty-one months).
2 years	*The spurt in word development.* Many conventional words appear in the child's vocabulary, which increases from 300 to 400 words at twenty-four to twenty-seven months to 1000 words at thirty-six months. He produces two- and three-word utterances, phrases, and sentences in which the pivot-open structure is well established.
	A given word can be used with a number of intonations, specifically, declarative ("doll."); emphatic ("doll!"); and interrogative ("doll?").
3 years	*The sentence period.* At thirty-six to thirty-nine months, the child can use 1000 words; he uses sentences containing grammatical features that anticipate the adult's use of language rules. He uses functionally complete sentences—that is, sentences that clearly designate an idea, as in the sentence, "This one riding horse"—that are grammatically incomplete.
3 to 5 years	The child uses sentences of all types: non-understandable sentences, functionally complete but grammatically incomplete sentences, simple sentences, simple sentences with phrases, compound sentences, complex sentences, and compound-complex sentences.
5 years to maturity	The individual's language system shows more frequent use of sentences with complex structure, increases in the variety of types of sentences, and increases in the length of sentences.

From F. J. Di Vesta. *Language, Learning, and Cognition.* Monterey, CA: Brooks/Cole (1974). Used with permission of the author.

An important contribution of modern psycholinguists has been the discovery that three-year-old children have learned most of the basic rules for the production of language. A native tendency to learn the language was hypothesized. It was called the "language acquisition device" or LAD (McNeill, 1970). With minimal amounts of exposure to language, the child seemingly learns most of the grammar–an acquisition independent of "intellectual" level. Since this outcome appears in a wide variety of cultures, the language-learning tendency is said to be universal (Lenneberg, 1967).

The infant attends to speech sounds as significant stimuli and acquires the phonological components (in the babbling stage, at about six months) and the basic grammatical components (at about three years). Regardless of intellectual ability or culture, an important part of the ability to acquire speech is innate; that is, because of inborn neural organization, speech "noises" that are grammatically related sound like language and not just haphazard sequences of noises. The similarity of grammars across cultures (some estimate as much as 80 percent) implies a possible universal basis in human infants for organizing the general principles of language. However, there are also differences in languages among cultures (the remaining 20 percent). These variations are presumed to be the ones that have to be learned. A main part of this chapter is devoted to how such variations are influenced by communication patterns in the child's home.

Adult–Child Interaction

Language development, social development, and cognitive development are complexly intertwined. Mother–infant interaction, responsiveness, and early encouragement of achievement is related to later achievement striving; frequent interaction with the child leads to the child's sense of trust and enjoyment in the environment. Helping the child to organize the environment leads to facilitation of progression from one cognitive level (sensorimotor) to another (pre-operational) (Gully, 1982).

An important part of language development is the nature of the interaction between a parent and child (Gleason, 1977; Lieven, 1978) since the parent depends on turn-taking feedback. At first, the parent (mother) will respond to many different types of "utterances," whether a yawn, cooing, or even a burp. With increasing participation in conversation by the infant that comes with increasing age, the infant is given more of a role in the interchange. By the middle of the second year (eighteen months), a conversational quality can be detected in the interaction. In this interchange, support is provided by the parent to encourage the child to maintain the conversation. Questions are asked, prompts are used, and feedback is supplied at the very early ages of six to eight months or earlier. The parent seems interested in maintaining conversational flow, even during the first few years, despite the child's limited lexicon and linguistic ability.

The characteristics of the child's language "theory" are the results of linguistic inputs from the world of speech around him/her (Malone and Guy, 1982). In the early formative years (chronological age from birth to three or four years old), the parents are primary sources of input. Further, some investigators have assumed that the mother's influence is greater than that of the father (Farwell, 1975). Others (Gleason, 1975) argue that the father provides a link with features of the environment (e.g., the world of work) not typically experienced by the child.

Despite these contrasting views, three characteristics emerge about the child's language development: (a) the only basis for constructing language is the speech the infant hears (Snow, 1972a, 1972b); (b) the primary sources of early contacts with speech are those provided by the parents; and (c) the quality of mothers' and fathers' speech differs. We can conclude that children in single parent homes will hear different patterns of linguistic inputs—thereby affecting their language system—depending on which parent provides the greater amount of linguistic interaction.

Father- and Mother-Talk

The parent adjusts his/her speech to express ideas familiar to the child. It is important for comprehension to form a link with the child's knowledge structures by basing the interaction on ideas familiar to the child. Contexts for target concepts or specific situations toward which the conversation is directed are typically explicit. Statements such as, "I think we'll get you dressed for school (or play)" and "Yes, that is a cat" are examples. Such statements convey ideas about the function of utterances and social conventions in contexts that are usable by the young language user. All adults—parents and other caregivers—produce modifications in their conversation that adapt to the level of the child yet provide challenges needed for further advances in language development. Nevertheless, all adults are not equally sensitive to the child's language code. Some adults speak below the child's level, thereby hindering language development. Other adults speak too much above the child's level, thereby disrupting the maintenance of conversational flow while also hindering language development. Either condition is less than optimal. Interestingly, the child seems to be most interested in responses slightly above his/her own level of development (Shipley, Smith, and Gleitman, 1969).

The specific role of the father in the child's acquisition of language is not clear. The reason is that very little research on father–infant influence has been conducted. Most research has been conducted on maternal influence. Nevertheless, there are several known characteristics of the relation of the father to the child that may have implications for language acquisition in father-absent homes (see Hummel, 1982, for example). These seem especially important despite the tendency to study mother– infant rather than father–infant interaction. Important in the father– child interaction is the finding that the child's preference for one parent over another changes, thereby providing opportunity for becoming acquainted with different kinds of experiences (Lamb, 1976, 1977a, 1977b). For example, interactions with the mother involve caregiving and routine function whereas the principal interaction with the father is that of play (Lamb, 1975, 1976, 1977a). Fathers tend to interact at the "play" level whether or not they are in primary or secondary caregiver roles. Obviously, interchanging of parental preferences is not possible in single parent homes.

Language patterns of mothers and fathers with infants and children do vary. In traditional homes and natural language environments (as opposed to laboratory settings), the mother sometimes seems to be the primary contributor to the linguistic environment. In one investigation (Friedlander, Jacobs, Davis, and Wetstone, 1972), two families were observed. In both families, the mothers' interactions were in English. However, in one family the father's interactions were mainly in Spanish. The infant at age two had learned some of the basic rudiments of Spanish, indicating the contribution of fathers to language development. On the other hand, a mother's comprehension of her own children's language is better than that of the father, although family members understand their child's language better than do non-family members. Conversely, mothers comprehend speech of other parents' children better than fathers; fathers were no better than non-parents in understanding children not related to them. One might reason that this complexly interrelated set of findings may be explained by the fact that maternal speech has greater intonational detail. Although it is simplified, it expresses variety and richness, making the child more attentive and responsive (Snow, 1972a; Brown and Hanion, 1970). Greater attentiveness by the child, in turn, results in more opportunities for the mother to understand what the child is saying.

Typically, fathers are less sensitive than mothers to: (a) changes in the child's language growth with age, (b) the child's interests, and (c) the child's speech. Although the father is typically less sensitive than the mother to subtle cues in the child's language, fathers tend not to involve the child in their own speech in the traditional home (Brown, 1973). This may not be a hindering factor because the child must still learn to adapt his/her communication to that of the father (Weist and Kruppe, 1977). To be effective, the speaker must be sensitive to the listener.

With regard to the semantic content of language, the father may also serve as the language contact with the outside world. Although fathers and mothers use a similar number of utterances, fathers' utterances are shorter (Malone and Guy, 1982), tending to be directed toward controlling the listener (child), directing the listener's behavior, and exerting his authority – imperatives that reflect control orientation and power of the speaker (Gleason, 1975). By implication, the quality of language development (communicating with individuals insensitive to cues and so on) may be retarded when the father and/or surrogates are missing.

Language Structures in Communicating with the Child

Although exposure to the speech of only a single parent of either sex may limit the nature of the linguistic input received by the child, there is an optimistic note. Dale (1972) surmises that the importance of parental speech in language development may be overestimated since infants and children rarely are exposed to only the speech of parents. The child receives much input from peers, older children, and other adults. Even older children tend, like adults, to adjust the level of their speech to that of the children with whom they speak (Shatz and Gelman, 1973); for example, four-year-olds without siblings are sensitive to the need for making adjustments when speaking to younger children (Sachs and Devin, 1976). The importance of simplification is seen in the finding that infants as young as one year old prefer to listen to a mother–child conversation than to a mother–adult conversation (Spring, 1974; Snow, 1972a, 1972b). Unless the child listens, the opportunity to experience adult language is lessened.

What Is Communicated in Adult–Child Conversations

Another trend in studying language emphasized the linguistic *structure* and the *semantic quality* of the language inputs to the child on the one hand, to the *meanings* and the *communicative properties* of the child's utterances, along with the growing *ability* of the child to communicate meanings to another on the other hand. These characteristics are reflected in the fact that the same surface structure of a child's utterance may have many underlying meanings, depending on context (Bloom, 1970). For example, "Mommy shoe" could mean "The shoe belongs to my mother" or "There is my shoe" or "That is a shoe" or "Is that a shoe?" depending on the meaning to be conveyed in the context of a given situation.

The analysis of communicative characteristics can be viewed in terms of adult-to-child and child-to-adult conversations. Of course, the child has access to, and can listen to, adult-to-adult conversations as part of his/her experience. Presumably, imitation of these patterns influences language development and is intrinsically part and parcel of language communications in all families. The extent and quality of the communication to which the child is exposed or in which the child is engaged depends on environmental opportunities, interaction within the family and with caregivers and peers, and, of course, television and other noninteractive media. Interactive communication with the child may be *directive* and *nonpersonal* (e.g., Johnny, go play; don't bother me); it may be *reflective*, at the same level of the child's communication pattern (e.g., repetitive baby talk). The nature of the primary linguistic data in adult–child interaction differs from adult–adult communication in (as summarized by Hummel, 1980, 1982, and others):

(a) Kinds of terms used (more familial representations, names of games, concrete objects, etc.)

(b) Active (motion) versus static verbs (more active verbs)

(c) Phonological simplification (lengthening of vowels)

(d) Prosody (e.g., the deliberate slowing down of speaking and lengthening of pauses between words and important grammatical phrases)

(e) Attentional inflections (raising pitch is often used to address the child to get or to hold attention)

(f) Whispering and increasing terminal pitch in interrogatives (these apparently oppositional prosodic cues, employed more frequently in adult–child speech than in adult–adult speech, may serve the function of holding attention)

(g) Mean length of utterance (shorter)

(h) Grammar (fewer inflections, verbs, false starts, imperfections such as broken sentences or incomplete sentences, more imperatives, more repetitions, more interrogatives, and more communication about objects and events in the present rather than past or future)

(i) Cognitive content [fewer ideas, use of questions that can be answered with a single word (yes/no, rather than wh_____ questions), and more expansions, repetitions, paraphrasing, and recasting of ideas].

Elaboration and Nonverbal Strategies

A widely-accepted approach to language development and consequent instruction is *modelling*. Through exposure to modelling, the child develops language competency (Cazden, 1965). Using *elaboration*, the adult expands and enriches the child's statements thus:

Child: "Doggie run."
Adult: "Yes, the brown dog is running after the cat."

The modelling of standard syntax, thus, is designed to assist the child's: (a) vocabulary, (b) word order, (c) grammatical development, and (d) expression and inflection usage.

Blount (1981) incorporated and expanded Cazden's theory and techniques, developing another approach that incorporated environmental stimuli of interest to the child. Using the *deictic utterances* (those that point to an object and name it), the adult points to objects which are colorful, novel, or otherwise of interest to the child. For instance:

adult (pointing to a daisy): That's a daisy.
(point to stem): See the long, green stem!
(point to petals): See the white, soft petals.
(point to center): Touch the round, yellow center.

Children who are exposed to deictic utterances seem to benefit in development and syntax; both the lexicon and use of noun phrases improves and increases. Cazden (1965) and Blount (1981) were supporters of the contemporary approaches to language development—those which rely upon social and psychological methods in order to enhance linguistics through a semantic, continual approach.

A similar approach to that of Blount (1981) is that of Werner and Kaplan (1964) who advocated use of the *gesture* in order to teach new vocabulary words to language-handicapped youngsters. For some children, at least temporarily, the gestures and the facial expression are the main modes of communication possible. Test scores reveal that the gesture is an effective means of communication (Werner and

Kaplan, 1964). Through the gesture, the child learns an autonomous medium of expression; the path for later learning of related words, phrases, and sentences is cleared. Three types of gestures are delineated:

(1) *Enactive gesture:* actions upon objects or with objects (e.g., catch fish, ride bike, comb hair)
(2) *Expressive gesture:* actions showing feelings and intentions (e.g., hand over mouth, shuffling, arms extended)
(3) *Depictive gesture:* actions depicting a static property of the object itself (e.g., bird = two fingers; tree = upright arm; swaying branches = moving hand)

As the adult communicates with the child using the enactive, expressive, or depictive gesture, he or she facilitates the child's vocabulary word acquisition and comprehension.

Some children (e.g., culturally or educationally "advantaged" children) accomplish the challenging but necessary task of vocabulary acquisition far more easily than others (Zivin, 1979). The single parent child is confronted with a more difficult task. A vocabulary enrichment program may be a necessary component of early language programs for single parent children. Lacking proper vocabulary skills, the single parent child is deficient in: (a) describing objects; (b) social and expressive tool usage; and (c) communicating, in general, with others (Zivin, 1979). Zivin recommended using adult modelling and learning task initiation for optimum language learning by the child; the adult responds to the child's language utterances by initiating simultaneous, related *activities* which the child then performs. For example, the adult supplies a toy car when the child states, "Car go bye-bye." A conversation about the characteristics of cars, then, accompanies the adult's and child's manipulation of the toy car. Bates (1979) advocated teaching young children words for objects upon which actions are performed—doll, shoe, bottle, cup, car. From *specific* word learning, the child advances to understanding and recognizing *general* classes of words (toys, clothing, containers, travel); conceptual abilities, therefore, expand.

Bates, in agreement with Cazden (1965), maintained that *imitation* was an optimal strategy in lexical language acquisition. As the adult notes words and phrases that have just begun to appear in the child's speech, the adult repeats the words and expands the length of the phrases or sentences. The child is interested in and able to readily imitate slightly higher level speech forms. The challenging levels have been primarily internalized already; thus, the imitated levels expand the child's language ability to produce the new structures (words, phrases, etc.) autonomously.

Bandura (1977) strongly supported the adult-modelling and child-observing recommendations of Zivin (1979) and Bates (1979); through observing and modelling adult behaviors, the child's motivation to achieve is increased. Social interactions with peers and adults further increase the child's social (e.g., perspective-taking and role-taking) and language skills (Bandura, 1977; Piaget, 1959).

Conversational Quality: Recasting

Parental adjustments, *recasting,* to the utterances of children from one to four or five years of age, is related to children's linguistic advances. These utterances are relatively easy for teachers and parents, whatever their status, to monitor. Nelson and his colleagues (Nelson, Bonvillian, Denninger, Kaplan, and Baker, 1984) in an interesting analysis of adult (maternal) adjustments arrived at a specification of the linguistic characteristics of the child's utterances that warrant attention. These specifications correspond to several presented in the aforegoing presentation. However, Nelson emphasized the importance of the quality of parental recasting of the child's utterances. Among the important kinds of recastings of the utterances are (Nelson et al., p. 41):

(1) Provide challenging but not out of reach *recasts* of the structural form of the child's utterances. For example, the child might say, "It broke," and the mother replies, "The cup fell off the table and broke." A simpler *recast* would be, "The cup broke." The parent can continue with a topic initiated by the child by providing a new sentence or by using a structural change with the same thread of meaning. The recasts also contribute to progress in the child's use of syntax.

(2) Adjust the communication situation such that the child will be able to link the situation to the conversation. By knowing what to attend to and knowing how to make sense out of the social context in which the conversation is taking place, the child readily incorporates language into his or her familiar tangible world.

(3) Adjust the child's strategies as much as possible. The same strategy for making replies may not have the same effect for all children. It is best to match the parent's style with the child's style. For example, when the child says, "Mine," the mother may reply, "Yes, the ball is yours," or more simply, "Yours?" The adult needs to carefully observe the child's reactions to various strategies. Vocabulary adjustments, topic continuation, and topic changes comprise the major adult strategies. The child's attention, re-

plies, and comprehension when each of the strategies are used determine the appropriateness of the respective strategy in a given situation. Repeated exposure to situation-appropriate strategies assists the child in cognitions and language advances.

The important concern is not with simple inputs or elaborations by the parent. Rather, the critical factor is integrating the child's readiness with inputs that challenge the child's linguistic level. When the child is challenged, these inputs permit the child to maintain attention and to make sense out of the information in an easy and effortless manner (see also Brown and Hanlon, 1970; Snow, 1972b). Furthermore, the adult inputs allow the corpus of communication to be extended or changed as befits the social context. Exposure only to simple baby talk for the first few years of life would clearly limit the child's language development. Conversely, the young child, as linguist, would promptly shut out an adult who conversed at the level of a newscaster. Some optimal level of complexity is necessary to attract the attention of the child to utterances if speech is to provide a basis for understanding experiences.

Baker and Nelson (1985), in another study, provide clear-cut evidence that deficiencies in children's use of various grammatical classes of words and syntactical forms are *not* due to limited cognitive development; rather the limitations are due to lack of *experience* with given forms of input. Thus, concern for appropriate inputs is necessary for the facilitation of language advances. As the adult recasts the child's utterances, increased opportunities for the child to analyze the use of a word in syntactical contexts and to test tentative production rules are available. Part of the effect of recasting may be due simply to the child's modelling which also provides increased experience with complex language forms. However, sheer imitation does not provide a sufficient explanation for language advances; only recasting would allow the child to compare his/her utterances with other, more complex conversational utterances on the same topic (Baker and Nelson, 1984). As Baker and Nelson indicate, "Recasting triggers syntactic advances." Thus, alterations sensitive to the quality of young children's comments are essential to advances in language ability.

The Interactive Roles of Language and Social Skills

Theorists and researchers have established that language skills are related to the child's emotional and social adjustment (Piaget,

1959; Vygotsky, 1962; Bandura, 1977). Language is described as the product of a continuous, reciprocal interaction between the child and the environment; the environment influences the behavior and the behavior, in turn, influences the environment (Bandura, 1977). Therefore, language has an important influence on the child. The single parent family provides a different interactive environment than does the traditional family. Consequently, the child's use of language for structuring the environment will also be modified.

Socialization is the vehicle whereby language development transpires and is able to flourish (Luria and Yudovick, 1959). Conversely, language facilitates socialization. Nemoianu (1980) viewed language development as a spiral phenomenon. Thought, overt behaviors, socialization, and language are described as interdependent; a quantitative gain in any one of the areas triggers a similar gain in another area, as the figure below illustrates.

Two requirements are present in order for the child from the nontraditional home to reach his or her full language potential: (a) the child has the ability (i.e., language) to interact and (b) the child is motivated to interact (i.e., the child has a receptive social climate) (Taylor, 1977). Language and socialization, then, are interdependent functions for enhanced learning and emotional adjustment for the single parent child.

The importance of language from Piaget's (1959) view is reflected in the role attributed to speech as "a window to the mind"; he maintained that thought precedes speech and that, through observing the child's speech and actions, an accurate assessment of the child's level or stage of cognitive development is possible. Language transforms thought by calling upon a more advanced schematization and a more mobile abstracting ability.

The opportunity for motor activity is frequently an important prerequisite or accompaniment to language (Luria and Yudovick, 1959). Literal speech, abstract language, and, later, symbolization with objects and gestures evolve as a result of the child's actions. As stage-

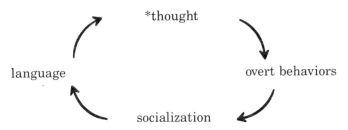

*thought

language

overt behaviors

socialization

*Starting point is optional.

like changes occur for the child in his or her egocentric speech (i.e., speech about oneself), silent planning and thinking eventuate. Later, through private or self-regulating speech, the child irons out inconsistencies and communicates more clearly—first to himself and later to others.

From this framework, parental speech patterns, in both traditional and nontraditional families, establish the groundwork for children's behavior in discovering language and its appropriate use (Blount, 1981). Children from "advantaged" homes (i.e., two parent families in which the socioeconomic level is above the average level) manifest very different behavioral and speech patterns from children of disadvantaged homes. Advantaged children differ in the following ways when compared to disadvantaged children: (a) they speak more; (b) they use more vocabulary words; (c) they use longer and more complex sentences; and (d) they use more parts of speech, more objects, and more labeling. Behaviorally, disadvantaged children (largely, perhaps, as a result of parent–child interaction patterns) show more: (a) bossiness, (b) hyperactivity, (c) over-excitement, or (d) extreme passivity (Bronfenbrenner, 1975). Probable reasons for the limited word knowledge and behavioral patterns of disadvantaged children are: (a) their limited experience with particular words and resultant category association disability, (b) their relatively limited and/or different home environments, child–parental interactions and experiences, and (c) the emergence of divorce or parental separation-related fears and tensions.

The interesting results of a recent study indicate that the single parent child orally responds more imaginatively than the dual parent child on "reality versus make-believe" assessments (Yawkey and Yawkey, 1983). The single parent child who is frequently more vulnerable to the anxieties of reality may escape by manually and verbally restructuring, temporarily, his/her world through the channel of imagination (Singer, 1973; Axline, 1967).

Presently, the large majority of single parent homes are economically disadvantaged (Lamb, 1982). Children from single parent families are also socially and/or emotionally "at risk," at least temporarily. Societal facilitation of the language, social, and emotional environment for the single parent child, then, becomes an ever-increasing priority.

Imitation

In virtually all broadly based discussions of social and language development (where social interchange, as in communication and dialogue, are present), some attention is given to the process of imitation, sometimes called modelling behavior. In some discussions (e.g., social learning), imitation appears as a most dominant mechanism of learning whereas in others (e.g., language learning) its role is seen as a more motivational influence than as a mechanism of learning. Nevertheless, as the child is exposed to language forms and social behaviors of others, he/she observes (i.e., hears or sees) these inputs and acts upon them in some way, whether by following, leading, or imitating language and other social actions.

Basic principles of imitation (Bandura, 1977) revolve around the question of "Who is imitated?" Such principles address whether or not particular language models will be imitated. In general, the influential model (the one imitated) displays at least three characteristics: (a) demonstrates exemplary or successful language behavior, (b) relates in an influential way to the learner, and (c) uses language in a manner that is within the behavioral competency (level) of the learner. Underlying these three principles, of course, is the understanding that each factor functions from the viewpoint of the learner, i.e., whether or not the learner *perceives* the model as influential or successful. It does not matter if the model is unsuccessful by objective standards. It is only important that he/she is *seen* as successful by the learner. Each of these factors will be discussed briefly.

Expertise

First, the imitated model seems to have the language conceptualizations or skills needed in a given situation. The model gets along with others, knows the language or dialect needed for a given cultural setting, competently executes a given skill, or achieves his/her goals. An important criterion often used implicitly is that other "successful people" (as defined by the observer) use similar behaviors (e.g., colloquialisms, vernacular, etc.) as does the model. Simply speaking, the "model as expert" seems, to the observer who imitates, to have good ideas and to do the right things at the right time. "Success" is to reach one's goals.

Power

Second, a model uses explicit methods to exert influence and has the power to provide or withdraw support. In other words, the model has rewarding capabilities; encouraging, rewarding, and supporting others' behaviors are witnessed by the observer.

Correspondence of Self-Concepts of Model and Observer

Third, children or others tend not to imitate language or other behaviors beyond their competencies. Observers select models who are perceived to be like themselves. More abstractly, models are selected whose behaviors, if imitated, will enhance the observer's self-concept. If the behavior imitated is outside the realm of competency, the behavior (language or other) will be reconstructed by the observer at his/her own structural level. This change is quite obvious in adult-to-child utterances as in the following examples modified slightly from many given by Brown and Bellugi (1964):

Adult Utterances	**Child's Imitative Utterances**
Jim will be unhappy.	Jim unhappy.
No, you can't write your name on Bill's shoe.	Write Bill shoe.

In the imitation process different models are selected for different subject matter domains. Similarly, the observer-learner-child is not equally competent in all imitated activities. The mother may model effective language patterns. However, the child's older peers frequently provide more influential social models. It is obvious that the child's imitative behaviors emerge from associations with a variety of language and social role models. We turn now to another process closely linked to imitation—that of identification. The importance of imitation and identification as they affect language and social behaviors is discussed throughout this chapter.

Gender Identification

Identification refers to the interpersonal relationships and situations in which one person serves as a lasting influence over another (Kagan and Phillips, 1968). The role of identification is a significant one because the establishment of certain, select relationships results in substantial changes in the child's personality (Lee, 1976). At approximately five years of age, the child's gender conception predicts the nature of his/her ultimate functioning in society (Kohlberg, 1966). The child's roles—the social behaviors and language patterns—are a direct result of the continual imitation of the same-sex role model and the consequent social reinforcement for these behaviors (Hetherington and Deur, 1975).

In consideration of the rapidly changing family structure in today's society, consequent changes in male and female role behaviors are predictable. For instance, one-third of the nation's children live in homes without at least one of their biological parents. Half of the preteenage children of divorce have not seen their fathers in over one year's time (Press, Clausen, Burger, and Abramson, 1983). The current statistics indicate that the availability of language and social role models for both sexes is often, at best, sporadic. Complete absence of at least one same-sex parent role model is an increasingly common phenomenon.

It is extremely difficult to decipher the relative effect of the child's biological make-up, environmental influences, and cognitive potential or development on his/her eventual acquisition of language and social skills. Research studies are necessarily limited and inconclusive because of the elusive nature of the variables which interactively influence the child at any given time.

Sex Typing: Behaviors and Attitudes

Practically from the moment of birth, children are surrounded by sex-typical stimuli and expectations for behaviors that the culture promotes for males and females. This cultural process is called *sex typing* or the process of learning appropriate masculine or feminine behaviors. Sex typing is especially influenced by the forces of the culture, media, peers, and parents during early childhood (Lefrancois, 1983).

Male and female behavior patterns, job roles, and stereotypes in the American society have recently undergone drastic changes. However, a set of markedly different characteristics still typifies males and females. A strong consensus across age, religion, marital status, and educational level was found among adults who described their perceptions of "typical" masculine and feminine traits (Ripple, Biehler, and Jaquish, 1982). Masculine traits were uniformly characterized as competent, rational, and assertive while female traits were warm, sensitive, empathic, and expressive. Parents typically provide daughters with less reinforcement for independent and aggressive behaviors. They are more protective of their female than their male offspring. Males are encouraged to develop their spatial–visual abilities through independent exploration while females are reinforced for exhibiting more peaceful, conforming, and affiliative behaviors (Maccoby and Jacklin, 1974). As a result of society's attitudinal differences for girls and boys, parents continue to treat boys and girls very differently.

Same versus Opposite Sex Parent

The extent to which the sex of the custodial parent affects the language and social development of the child is debatable. Until recently, data that indicated the effects on children of same sex versus different sex custody were very limited. Contemporary research studies have yielded some interesting findings. Data suggest that girls in the custody of single fathers may have more marked adjustment problems than boys with single fathers (Santrock, Warshak, and Elliott, 1982). Earlier research indicated that, for boys, interpersonal and social adjustment was most difficult when the mother was the custodian (Hetherington et al., 1982). In same sex match of boys and fathers, boys show more competent social behavior in stepfather families than girls in stepfather families and boys in mother-custody families (Santrock et al., 1982). Girls in mother-custody families display more competent social behavior than girls in stepfather families (Santrock et al., 1982). These pieces of research do not provide conclusive evidence of custodial sex effects on children. Some literature indicates that children do not require the presence of the same sex parents in the family to develop appropriate sex-role behavior. Children of both sexes in single female-headed or single male-headed families may develop normal levels of emotional stability and self-esteem (Cashion, 1982).

Because widespread media and parental bias continues for male and female role expectations, single parents are well advised to acquire a new set of perceptions and expectations about sex-role behaviors. Children from single parent families require teacher and parent encouragement to achieve a balance between "traditional girl" and "traditional boy" roles (Lamb, 1982). Girls and boys who reside with a single mother and, therefore, lack the exposure to a male role model may need to receive greater amounts of reinforcement and exposure from male role models in order to promote more assertive behaviors. Conversely, boys and girls who reside with single fathers may require encouragement from female role models for expressing increased sensitivity and a concern for relations with others. Thus, the content, conceptualizations, and patterns of language expression of the mother and father may differ drastically. The continued absence of one parent may result in the child's deprivation of exposure to those language characteristics critical to the development of communication and social skills.

Because of the ramifications of the child's emotional well-being upon subsequent social and language competency, additional studies exploring the respective effects of same sex and opposite sex parents are needed. It is hoped that future studies addressing children's imitation, sex-role modelling, parental identification, and language pattern development will answer many of the perplexing questions and contradictory findings.

Language and Play

Most adults have observed that play is the important occupation of children. Through play they develop language spontaneity and positive interpersonal interactions (Singer, 1973; Trostle, 1984). Teachers often serve as both planner and coordinator of the "child–child" happenings in the classroom (Nemoianu, 1980, p. 106) thereby facilitating the types of play that contribute to language and social development. Active learning through play is a most natural and promising route to word identification, vocabulary word development, and comprehension skills for the child who has a language-deficient home environment. The true key for promoting language development is intrinsic, residing in the child's "willingness" to communicate successfully (Nemoianu, 1980). Since play is typically self-generated and oriented toward the child's own goals, it is a natural medium for developing the child's willingness to develop communication skills. "The more sophisticated the children's (play and) games are, the more rapidly will their language abilities advance" (Nemoianu, 1980, p. 73). It behooves the caregiver to provide stimulating play environments; environments that allow for advanced communication requirements and challenging social interactions (making cooperative decisions, taking leadership roles, asking relevant questions, giving instructions, etc.). Language learning in these settings affects increasingly higher order and more language-conducive play behaviors.

The mutually supportive relationship between language and play affects affectivity through use of particular types of play. Children who role-play regularly use more positive affect and less fighting and hyperactive behavior (Axline, 1967; Trostle, 1984). Their behavior is more expressive, constructive, and goal-directed than that of children in situations without deliberate intervention. They use more parts of speech and more verbal communication (Smilansky, 1968; Singer, 1973).

Through findings such as those described, play training programs are given credibility for enhancing the single parent child's environment and for promoting his or her verbalization and adaptation skills. The quality and quantity of the child's fantasy play is correlated with: (a) greater verbal communication, (b) longer and more complex sentence usage, (c) more sensitivity responding to others' cues, (d) more spontaneity, (e) more creativity, (f) increased use of labeling, (g) greater attention span, and (h) more expression and emotion (Freyberg, 1973).

Garvey (1977) found similar relationships and advocated the use of specific play training methods adapted to the language and social and emotional readiness of an individual child. The use of increasingly complex play and elaboration was found to relate to language advances (Garvey, 1977; Axline, 1967). The implementation of verbal cue games, as well as games with a variety of self-controls, for promoting the child's language learning were advocated (Sutton-Smith, 1971).

Many single parent children are confronted with the problems of: (a) limited opportunities for socialization, (b) limited language interactions, (c) limited parental education levels, (d) poverty, and (e) frequent home transitions. Language learning by any method is thwarted when, for the child, any of the security or affiliation needs are unmet (Smith, 1981). Overcoming the single parent child's possible emotional maladjustment and home deficiencies requires special affective, economic, and social support systems. When such deficiencies exist, the appropriate guidance and remedial measures frequently alleviate or prevent possible language and social handicaps (Vasquez, 1979). Language skills (and reading) are highly significant factors in a child's school success (Smith, 1981). To ignore or neglect classroom or home applications of research on language achievement may prevent awareness of promising new directions for improving the single parent child's educational future.

Thought and emotional development, socialization, action, and language development for the single parent child are interdependent. An advance in one area, according to Taylor (1977), may precipitate improvement in other areas. Methods for enriching each of the four foundation components of adjustment for the single parent child include promotion of self-awareness and emotional well-being through such diverse means as play interactions, private speech, and working relationships. Each or all of the methods enables the child to gain an understanding of his or her own goals, behaviors, self-worth, and individuality.

Socialization and action are targeted through play groups, programs for language and word advancements, and a motor activity/ experience or discovery approach to learning. Language development, the final link, is the end result, as well as the facilitator, of the child's socialization, self-awareness, and behavior. Language is an influential key to later educational and social success of the single parent child. An attitude of compassion and active interest on the part of significant others—caregivers, teachers, and parents—is needed. With explicit control, such attitudes may assist the child from the single parent family in overcoming barriers to language learning and social integration.

The discussion presented in the preceding section emphasizes that whatever conversational input the child receives must arrive in a form usable by him/her if it is to provide a base from which the child can develop individualized discourse rules. Structured information not yet in the child's own language system is thereby provided that the child can code in relation to the existing structure (Nelson, 1980).

It is important that new syntactic information, and not mere expansions, be displayed in relation to the child's existing structures. For example, a reply of "The girls are running" to the child's utterance of "Girls run" is simply an expansion and provides no new structures; a reply of "The lively girls are running through the green field" provides new syntactic information as well as expanded content information. *How* adults speak to children is as important as *what* they say. Both facets are important considerations for educational and therapeutic programs directed toward helping children with difficulties in language mastery and toward helping parents understand their roles in modelling effective conversational input for normal children.

Summary

The child's early years, ranging from birth through approximately five years are considered the "formative years" (Bloom, 1964). The single parent plays a major role in insuring the availability of a multitude of language and social opportunities for the developing child. Swick and Manning (1983) suggest courses of action that fathers (and mothers) can follow in order to enrich the child's environment. A reduction in the often deleterious effects of single parenthood, therefore, becomes possible.

During infancy and early childhood, the single parent can respond, through verbalizations, gestures, and facial expressions, to the infant's utterances. Playing frequently and informally with the infant is recommended.

The preschool program exerts significant effects upon the child's language and social development. If the infant or toddler is enrolled in a child care center, the single parent needs to investigate: (a) the infant–caregiver ratio, (b) the physical surroundings, (c) the staff–center philosophy toward play and learning, and (d) the "curriculum" (Swick and Manning, 1983). Recent research indicates that the child's socialization and language development are closely related to the psychological atmosphere of the family (Lamb, 1975). The following recommendations are delineated for providing a healthy psychological atmosphere within the working couple or single parent child's home (Swick and Manning, 1983). They are directed at reinforcing and advancing the child's language and social skills. Recommendations include:

(1) Increase availability time; integrate task and job time into family time together.

(2) Spend creative, open-ended play times with the child.

(3) Set aside "private times" with the child on a regular basis; take time to read, discuss, question, observe, discover, investigate, play games, do homework, attend movies, cook, and write stories.

(4) Display affection toward the child in physical and social situations.

(5) Actively listen to your child; respond in a positive, encouraging manner; allow the child to lead the conversation frequently. Answer the child's questions thoroughly and enthusiastically. Elaborate the child's utterances and recast their structure and syntax.

(6) Pay close attention to your child's overall development on a daily basis. Consult the child's teacher, caregiver, and pediatrician regularly to check the child's physical, social, and academic growth.

(7) Take an active role in the child's education; become an active supporter of the child's classroom or child care center. Visit the classroom or center, perhaps, as a resource person or tutor. Insure that the facilities are attractive and stimulating, that the staff is knowledgeable and competent, and that the activities which are provided are safe, age-appropriate, and well-planned and executed.

(8) Provide appropriate and desirable social and language role models– both young and old, males and females–for the child. Peers and older children who serve as role models for the child influence the child's social and academic growth to a great extent; frequently, children glean more understanding and knowledge from same-age role models than from parents or other adults.

(9) Read to the child on a daily basis. Discuss what you have read. Ask questions that relate the story to an event in the child's life. Have the youngster retell the story in his/her own words. Later, assist the child in realistic or creative writing about the story.

(10) Talk to the child frequently about his/her feelings; feelings of frustration, fear, loneliness, anger, joy, and surprise are universal. As the child discusses these feelings, he or she learns to: (a) recognize the existence of the feelings, (b) deal with the feelings, and (c) extend vocabulary word repertoire through labeling the feelings.

(11) Use tape recorders, records, educational television, and film-strips or movies as the basis for the child's oral language development. Become actively involved in these experiences along with the child. Follow up each activity with related writing, discussion, questioning, or drawing opportunities.

(12) Invite neighborhood children to the child's home on a regular basis. Provide a variety of language-stimulating games, toys, puppets, and dress-up clothing for the groups or dyads.

(13) Provide homemade and commercial language games for the child, such as *Boggle, Password, Spill and Spell, Scrabble, Trivial Pursuit for Juniors,* simple crossword puzzles, and hidden word searches.

(14) Assist the child in preparing a word book or diary. Each day the youngster records his/her new words and the day's events in a sequential fashion. If the child desires, encourage and reinforce his/her efforts by listening and responding to the child later as he reads his words, sentences, or diary entries.

(15) Investigate the local social support agencies in the community, such as YMCA, YWCA, Girl Scouts, Boy Scouts, and Big Brother/Big Sister programs. Valuable role modeling opportunities, as well as learning and academic growth experiences, are provided, implicitly, by these organizations.

(16) Allow the child a great deal of time to "learn by doing." Provide opportunities for exploration, experimentation, and discovery within the child's school, home, and recreational environment.

In conclusion, this chapter has emphasized the importance of promoting the child's language and social skills. Models and challenges for the single parent child provide the support necessary in a rapidly changing society—one characterized by a decline in secure attachments and by increasing expectations for children to function in demanding, adult-like roles (Umansky, 1983). Participation in symbolic play activities, communication with adults, exposure to a variety of role models, and the like all contribute to the single parent child's comprehension of narratives and conversation and, ultimately, to language and social development.

References

ADAMS, G. R. "The Effects of Divorce: Outcome of a Preschool Intervention Program," paper presented at the Annual Meeting of the American Educational Research Association, New York, New York (March 19–23, 1982).

AXLINE, V. M. *Play Therapy.* New York:Ballentine Books (1967).

BAKER, N. D. and K. E. Nelson. "Recasting and Related Conversational Techniques for Triggering Syntactic Advances by Young Children," *First Language,* 5:3–22 (1984).

BANDURA, A. "The Role of Modeling Processes in Personality Development," in *The Young Child,* W. W. Hartup and N. L. Smothergill, eds., Washington, DC:National Association for the Education of Young Children (1967).

BANDURA, A. *Social Learning Theory.* Englewood Cliffs, NJ:Prentice Hall (1977).

BATES, E. *The Emergence of Symbols.* New York: Academic Press (1979).

BELSKY, J., L. D. Steinberg, and A. Walker. "The Effects of Day Care," in *Nontraditional Families: Parenting and Child Development,* M. E. Lamb, ed., Hillsdale, NJ:Lawrence Erlbaum Associates, Inc. (1982).

BLOOM, B. S. *Stability and Change in Human Characteristics.* New York:John Wiley & Sons (1964).

BLOOM, L. *Language Development: Form and Function on Emerging Grammars.* Boston:MIT Press (1970).

BLOUNT, B. G. "The Development of Language in Children," in *Handbook of Cross-Cultural Human Development,* R. H. Munroe, R. L. Munroe, and B. B. Whiting, eds., New York:Garland Publishing, Inc. (1981).

BRONFENBRENNER, U. *Influences on Human Development.* New York:Holt, Rinehart, and Winston, Inc. (1975).

BROWN, R. and C. Hanlon. "Derivational Complexity and Order of Acquisition in Child Speech," in *Cognition and the Development of Language,* J. R. Hayes, ed., New York:John Wiley & Sons (1970).

BROWN, R. *A First Language.* Cambridge, MA:Harvard University Press (1973).

BROWN, R. and U. Bellugi. "Three Processes in the Child's Acquisition of Syntax," *Harvard Educational Review,* 34:133–151 (1964).

CASHION, B. G. "Female-Headed Families: Effects on Children and Clinical Implications," *Journal of Marital and Family Therapy,* 8(2):77–85 (April, 1982).

CAZDEN, C. "Environmental Assistance to the Child's Acquisition of Grammar," Unpublished doctoral dissertation, Harvard University (1965).

DALE, P. S. *Language Development: Structure and Function* (2nd ed.). New York:Holt, Rinehart, & Winston (1972).

DI VESTA, F. J. *Language, Learning and Cognitive Processes.* Monterey, CA: Brooks/Cole (1974).

EIDUSON, B. T., M. Kornfein, I. L. Zimmerman, and T. S. Weisner. "Comparative Socialization Practices in Traditional and Alternative Families," in *Nontraditional Families: Parenting and Child Development,* M. E. Lamb, ed., Hillsdale, NJ: Lawrence Erlbaum Associates, Inc. (1982).

FARWELL, C. "The Language Spoken to Children," *Human Development,* 18:288–309 (1975).

FREYBERG, J. T. "Increasing the Imaginative Play of Urban Disadvantaged Kindergarten Children Through Systematic Training," in *The Child's World of Make-Believe,* J. L. Singer, ed., New York:Academic Press (1973).

FRIEDLANDER, B. Z., A. C. Jacobs, B. B. Davis, and H. S. Wetstone. "Time-sampling Analysis of Infants' Natural Environments in the Home," *Child Development,* 43:730–740 (1972).

GARVEY, C. *Play.* Cambridge, MA:Harvard University Press (1977).

GLEASON, J. B. "Fathers and Other Strangers: Men's Speech to Young Children," in

Developmental Psycholinguistics: Theory and Application, D. Dato, ed., Washington, DC:Georgetown University, pp. 289–297 (1975).

GLEASON, J. B. "Talking to Children: Some Notes on Feedback," in *Talking to Children: Language Input and Acquisition*, C. Snow and C. Ferguson, eds., New York:Cambridge University Press, pp. 199–205 (1977).

GULLY, S. G. "The Relationship of Infant Stimulation to Cognitive Development," *Childhood Education*, 58(4):247–254 (1982).

HETHERINGTON, E. M., M. Cox, and R. Cox. "Effects of Divorce on Parents and Children," in *Nontraditional Families: Parenting and Child Development*, M. E. Lamb, ed., Hillsdale, NJ:Lawrence Erlbaum Associates, Inc. (1982).

HETHERINGTON, E. M. and J. L. Deur. "The Effects of Father Absence on Child Development," in *Influences on Human Development*, U. Bronfenbrenner and M. A. Mahoney, eds., New York:Holt, Rinehart & Winston, Inc. (1975).

HUMMEL, D. D. "The Role of the Father in the Language Acquisition Process," Unpublished doctoral dissertation, The Pennsylvania State University (1980).

HUMMEL, D. D. "Syntactic and Conversational Characteristics of Fathers' Speech," *Journal of Psycholinguistic Speech*, 11(5):465–484 (1982).

KADAR-SUGAR, J. "Influence of Social Environment on the Development of Verbal and Social Competence in Preschool Children," *Studia Psychologica*, 22(1):51–59 (1980).

KAGAN, J. K., and W. Phillips. "Measurement of Identification: A Methodological Note," in *Children: Readings in Behavior and Development*, E. D. Evans, ed., New York:Holt, Rinehart & Winston, Inc. (1968).

KOHLBERG, L. "A Cognitive-Developmental Analysis of Children's Sex-Role Concepts and Attitudes," in *The Development of Sex Differences*, E. E. Maccoby, ed., Stanford, CA:Stanford University Press (1966).

LAMB, M. G. "Forgotten Contributors to Child Development," *Human Development*, 18:245–266 (1975).

LAMB, M. G. *"The Role of the Father in Child Development,"* New York:Wiley (1976).

LAMB, M. G. "Father-Infant and Mother-Infant Interaction in the First Year of Life," *Child Development*, 48:167–181 (1977a).

LAMB, M. G. "The Development of Mother-Infant and Father-Infant Attachments in the Second Year of Life," *Development of Psychology*, 13:637–648 (1977b).

LAMB, M., ed. *Nontraditional Families: Parenting and Child Development*, Hillsdale, NJ:Lawrence Erlbaum Associates, Inc. (1982).

LEE, C. L. *Personality Development in Childhood*. Belmont, CA:Wadsworth Publishing Co., Inc. (1976).

LEFRANCOIS, G. R. *Of Children*. Belmont, CA:Wadsworth Publishing Co. (1983).

LENNEBERG, E. H. *The Biological Foundations of Language*. New York:John Wiley & Sons (1967).

LIEVEN, E. "Conversations Between Mothers and Young Children: Individual Differences and their Possible Implications for the Study of Language Learning," in *The Development of Communication*, N. Waterson and C. Snow, eds., New York: Wiley (1978).

LURIA, A. and F. Yudovick. *Speech and the Development of Mental Processes in the Child*. New York:Staples, Inc. (1959).

MACCOBY, E. E. and C. N. Jacklin. *The Psychology of Sex Differences*. Stanford, CA:Stanford University Press (1974).

MALONE, M. J. and R. F. Guy. "A Comparison of Mothers' and Fathers' Speech to Their Three-Year-Old Sons," *Journal of Psycholinguistic Research,* 11:599–608 (1982).

MCNEILL, D. *The Acquisition of Language: The Study of Developmental Psycholinguistics,* New York:Harper & Row, Inc. (1970).

MENYUK, P. *The Acquisition and Development of Language.* Englewood Cliffs, NJ:Prentice-Hall, Inc. (1971).

MOFIDI-FARKHONDEH. "Effects of Divorce and the Consequent Absence of One Parent on the Language Development of 3–5 Year Old Nursery School Children," *Dissertation Abstracts International,* 41(8-A):3461–3462 (1981).

NELSON, K. G. "Theories of the Child's Acquisition of Syntax: A Look at Rare Events and at Necessary, Catalytic, and Irrelevant Components of Mother-Child Conversation," in *Studies in Child Language and Multilingualism: Annals of the New York Academy of Science, Vol. 345,* V. Teller and S. J. White, eds., New York:The New York Academy of Science (1980).

NELSON, K. E., J. D. Bonvillian, M. S. Denninger, B. J. Kaplan, and N. D. Baker. "Maternal Input Adjustments and Non-Adjustments as Related to Children's Linguistic Advances and to Language Acquisition Theories," in *The Development of Oral and Written Language in Social Contexts,* A. D. Pelligrini and T. D. Yawkey, eds., Norwood, NJ:ABLEX Publishing Corp. (1984).

NEMOIANU, A. M. *The Boat's Gonna Leave. Pragmatics and Beyond.* Amsterdam:J. Benjamins (Series Number 1) (1980).

PIAGET, J. *The Language and Thought of the Child.* London:Lund Humphries (1959).

PRESS, A., P. Clausen, W. Burger, P. Abramson, J. McCormick, and S. Cavezos. "Divorce American Style," *Newsweek,* 101(2):42–48 (January 10, 1983).

RIPPLE, R. E, R. F. Biehler, and G. A. Jaquish. *Human Development.* Boston: Houghton Mifflin, Inc. (1982).

SACHS, J. and J. Devin. "Young Children's Use of Age-Appropriate Speech Styles in Social Interaction and Role-Playing," *Journal of Child Language,* 3:81–98 (1976).

SANTROCK, J. W., R. A. Warshak, and G. L. Elliott. "Social Development and Parent–Child Interaction in Father-Custody and Stepmother Families," in *Nontraditional Families: Parenting and Child Development,* M. E. Lamb, ed., Hillsdale, NJ:Lawrence Erlbaum Associates, Inc. (1982).

SCHATZ, M. and R. Gelman. "The Development of Communicative Skills. Modifications in the Speech of Young Children as a Function of Listener," *Monographs of the Society for Research in Child Development,* 38:152 (1973).

SHIPLEY, E. F., C. S. Smith, and L. R. Gleitman. "A Study in the Acquisition of Language: Free Responses to Commands," *Language,* 45:322–342 (1969).

SINGER, J. *The Child's World of Make-Believe.* New York:Academic Press, Inc. (1973).

SMILANSKY, S. *The Effects of Sociodramatic Play on Disadvantaged Preschool Children.* New York:Wiley (1968).

SMITH, C. W. "Uncle Dad," *Esquire,* 103(3):73–85 (March 1985).

SMITH, P. D. "A Review of the Research on the Teaching of Reading in Bilingual Education," ERIC ED 210 903, pp. 1–193 (October 9, 1981).

SNOW, C. E. "Mothers Speech to Children Learning Language," *Child Development,* 43:549–565 (1972a).

SNOW, C. E. "Young Children's Responses to Adult Sentences of Varying Complexity," paper presented to the 3rd International Congress of Applied Linguistics, Copenhagen (August 1972b).

SOPHIAN, C., ed. *Origins of Cognitive Skills.* Hillsdale, NJ:Lawrence Erlbaum Associates, Inc. (1984).

SPRING, D. R. "Effects of Style of Maternal Speech on Infant's Selection of Vocal Reinforcement," unpublished paper, University of Washington.

SUTTON-SMITH, B. "The Role of Play in Cognitive Development," in *Child's Play,* R. E. Herron and B. Sutton-Smith, eds., New York:John Wiley & Sons, Inc. (1971).

SWICK, K. J. and M. L. Manning. "Father Involvement in Home and School Settings," *Childhood Education,* 60(2):128–135 (1983).

TAYLOR, D. M. "Bilingualism and Intergroup Relations," in *Bilingualism,* P. A. Hornby, ed., New York:Academic Press, Inc. (1977).

TROSTLE, S. L. "An Investigation of the Effects of Child-Centered Group Play Therapy Upon Sociometric, Self-Control, and Play Behavior Ratings of Three- to Six-Year-Old Bilingual Puerto Rican Children," unpublished doctoral dissertation, The Pennsylvania State University, University Park, PA (1984).

UMANSKY, W. "On Families and the Re-Valuing of Childhood," *Childhood Education,* 59(4):259–266 (1983).

VASQUEZ, J. "Bilingual Education's Needed Third Dimension," *Educational Leadership,* 37:166–168 (1979).

VYGOTSKY, L. S. *Thought and Language.* Cambridge, MA:MIT Press (1962).

WEIST, R. M. and B. Kruppe. "Parent and Sibling Comprehension of Children's Speech," *Journal of Psycholinguistic Research,* 6:49–58 (1977).

WERNER, M. and B. Kaplan. *Symbol Formation.* New York:Wiley (1964).

YAWKEY, T. D. and M. L. Yawkey. "Assessing Young Children for Imaginativeness Through Oral Reporting: Preliminary Results," ERIC Document AN ED 231 547, RIE (1983).

ZIVIN, G., ed. *The Development of Self-Regulation Through Private Speech.* New York:John Wiley & Sons, Inc. (1979).

PART III

Personal Choices

IN THIS FINAL part of the text, we show that families can differ in complexity and by choice of the adults. Regardless of structure, complexity, and type, families can make contributions to the growth, development, and learning of children and to the family unit. Juan Ramon Morales-Flores highlights the choice factor in his chapter, "Fathers by Choice."

Across the chapter there are several linking concepts. They are: (a) gay fathers' choices to parent, (b) gay fathers' relationships with their children, and (c) issues surrounding gay fathers in our society. Each of these concepts is discussed in the following sections.

Gay Fathers' Choices for Parenting

Toward supporting gay fathers' choices for parenting, Morales-Flores distinguishes between lifestyles and fathering roles. Although these are two differing dimensions of life structures, current societal beliefs about the gay father traditionally tend to merge their lifestyles with fathering roles. Lifestyles of gays focus on sexual preferences and the degree to which gays have public (versus self) identities in accord with those behaviors. In this instance, Morales-Flores, using support data from researchers (e.g., Miller, 1979), describes four differing lifestyles of gay fathers: trade fathers, homosexual fathers, gay fathers, and publicly gay fathers. On the other hand, fathering roles focus on nurturing and caretaking of children. From results of research studies, gayness is viewed

167

as compatible with lifestyles but is not compatible with fathering roles.

Morales-Flores reports that greater numbers of gay fathers in divorce situations are seeking the custody of their children through the courts. In situations of divorce, problems with children occur largely because of parent separation and not because of sexual preferences of the gay parent. This is especially relevant and pertinent when the child knows about the lifestyle of the gay parent.

Using informal questionnaire data, Morales-Flores attempts to show that sexual preference of the gay parent does not have a negative effect on the children. In fact, sexual preference has little to do with parenting, and results of research data seem to support the gay father's desire and ability to parent (Riddle, 1977). First, the majority of gay individuals are reared in heterosexual families, and no evidence exists that gay parents rear greater numbers of children with gay preferences. Second, it appears that gay parents are more tolerant of children's preferences than heterosexual parents and attempt to support their children's own choices. Third, and according to Morales-Flores, gay parents, more than heterosexual parents, understand the necessity of having adult role models of both sexes for their children. Constant and systematic contact with family members of both sexes is important for children for the growth of primary role models. In sum, available research evidence seems to support the role of the gay father in parenting and his choice for parenting responsibilities.

Morales-Flores describes specific needs regarding gay fathers' choices for parenting. For example, greater recognition and awareness of the needs of gay couples by social welfare and mental health agencies and by our legal system are required. Rights and responsibilities of individuals should not be denied based on sexual preferences; gay fathers, too, need support of agencies and the legal system. In addition, there is a need for adoption agencies and foster homes to continue to consider gay couples as possible foster and adoptive parents.

Gay Father–Child Relations

Results of research studies (e.g., Miller, 1979) tend to show that gay father–child relationships improve when children are aware of their father's sexual preference and when they are gradually introduced to it. Morales-Flores notes that after disclosing their gayness, fathers tend to have better relationships with their children and also spend more time with them than before their disclosures. The honesty and disclosures between fathers and children may ultimately help strengthen relationships and at the same time provide better communication between them. In addition, honesty and disclosure between father and child tend to make the father a more positive figure for the children.

Children tend to accept disclosure of a father's gayness more readily than wives accept such a revelation from their husbands. In situations of divorce and a husband's disclosure of his gayness, many spouses attempt to prevent their children from continuing to see their father and may try to terminate father–child relationships. However, Morales-Flores reports that partial or complete termination of father–child relations appears to do greater harm than good to the child's growth and development and establishment of gender role identity. With the termination of unpleasant marriages, results of data seem to suggest that father–child relations tend to improve. These results are especially evident when gay fathers moved from the households into openly gay lifestyles.

Finally, in surveying the results from the Mayadas and Duehn (1976) study, Morales-Flores notes that the gay family was perceived by children and adolescents as much more supportive and growth-producing than the heterosexual family. Apparently children living in these gay families felt that their fathers were less authoritarian, more open, and more willing to discuss with them and support their endeavors than children living in heterosexual families. It is apparent that more research is needed to examine adult–child relationships and related complex variables within gay father households.

Issues Surrounding Gay Fathers

Morales-Flores points out that research on gay fathers is scanty at best. Additional studies need to be made to clarify several issues and misconceptions that exist in our society regarding gay fathers and their relationships with their children. Morales-Flores describes several of these issues and misconceptions. First, it is generally believed that all gay men and gay fathers demonstrate the same kinds of behaviors. Morales-Flores, in this instance, distinguishes between lifestyles and parenting behaviors and attempts to show distinctions between them. Second, the issue of whether gay fathers are positive role models for their children needs further examination. Available research evidence suggests that not only are gay fathers sound role models but that they may be more nurturant, supportive, and likely to provide more choices to their children than heterosexual fathers. Morales-Flores notes that gay fathers are more androgynous than heterosexual fathers and therefore expose their children to greater and more individual concepts of diversity.

Third, a common belief held by many individuals in our society is that gay fathers increase the amount of gayness in their children. Research evidence, however, suggests that gender identity, after being established, is resistant to change. In a related note, Morales-Flores explains that gender modelling for girls is more flexible than for boys because the former are reinforced for imitating same- and cross-sexed adults, whereas the latter are reinforced for modelling adults of their same sex.

Morales-Flores notes that further investigations will increase our understanding and hopefully, at the same time, reduce misconceptions about gay father parenting.

Conclusion

The ideas that families can differ by choice of adults and that they do make contributions to children's development regardless of their structure, complexity, and type are facts. The beliefs and issues associated with these current facts, however, require further examination and empirical investigation. These beliefs and issues are directly or indirectly associated with: (a) gay fathers' choices to parent, (b) gay fathers' relationships with their children, and (c) gay fathers and society.

As society continues its trek into the present and future, family types will continue to differ and increase in number. From a constructive child and family perspective, these personal choices and family types they produce will necessitate rethinking and further refining of traditional definitions of the family unit. They will require much further exploration of their contributions to their children's development, learning, and to society.

References

GARBARINO, J. *Children and Families in the Social Environment.* New York:Aldine Publishing Company (1982).

HETHERINGTON, E., M. Cox, and R. Cox. "Effects of Divorce on Parents and Children in Nontraditional Families," in *Parenting and Child Development*, M. E. Lamb, ed., New Jersey:Lawrence Erlbaum Associates, Inc., pp. 66–92 (1982).

MAYADAS, N. S. and W. D. Duehn. "Children in Gay Families: An Investigation of Services," *The Homo-sexual Counseling Journal,* 3(2):70.84 (1976).

MILLER, B. "Gay Fathers and Their Children," *The Family Coordinator,* 28(4): 544.552 (1979).

RIDDLE, D. I. "Gay Parents and Child Custody Issues" (Report No. C G012219), Tucson, AZ:University of Arizona, Psychology Department (ERIC Document Reproduction Service No. ED 147746) (1972).

SAFILIOUS-ROTHCHILD, C. "Parents' Needs for Child Care," in *Childcare: Who Cares?* P. Roby, ed., New York:Basic Books, pp. 37.45 (1973).

CHAPTER 8

Parents by Choice:
Gay Fathers

JUAN R. MORALES-FLORES

Introduction

ALONG WITH CHANGES in our society regarding socioeconomic aspects that have affected the family struture, the role of the father in recent years has come to be less stereotyped (Lamb, 1976; Chibucos and Kail, 1981; Collins, 1979; Saul, 1984). A few decades ago, it was not accepted that men would be involved in nurturing and caretaking of children (Robinson, 1981; Robinson, 1988), even less that gay fathers could be fit parents (Saul, 1984). However, current research in this area supports the position that fathers, when permitted, will be as nurturant with children as mothers (Belsky, 1979; Lamb, 1976). Also, fathers seem to establish a stimulating relationship with their children while taking care of them, resulting in cognitive and social stimulation (Radin, 1982; Sawin and Parke, 1979). Fathers seem to be capable of fulfilling attachment roles with their children, usually expected only from mothers (Chibucos and Kail, 1981). In addition to the changing role of the father, the structure of the family has been changed. There are more single parent families now than ever before (U.S. Census, 1988). Meanwhile, the number of fathers who obtain custody of their children is increasing (Collins, 1979; Saul, 1984). Also, due to gay awareness movements, it is more frequent that homosexual fathers are attempting to retain custody of their children. Although more information about the gay father is available in the 1980s than before (i.e., Bozett, 1980; Mayadas and Duehn, 1976; Miller, 1978; Miller, 1979; Riddle, 1977; Riddle, 1978; Saul, 1984; Wyers, 1987), there still remains much misunderstanding regarding the gay father and child relationship. In particular, the ability of gay men as fathers is still an issue.

In this chapter, the research literature is reviewed regarding gay fathers and their relationship with their children and the society. It is commonly believed in our society that gay men are not suitable as fathers (Miller, 1978; Miller, 1979; Riddle, 1977; Saul, 1984). However, for many years gay men have "successfully contributed to child rearing as surrogate parents: teachers, day-care personnel, scout leaders, ministers, policemen, guidance counselors, coaches, and pediatricians" (Miller, 1978, p. 250). It is also commonly believed that there is a great amount of homosexuality among gay fathers' children although there is no evidence that supports this contention (Miller, 1979). This issue, in addition to others, has been discussed in many situations including court settings and continues as a stereotype in society. Most of these misconceptions started to change with the help of the gay-liberation movements and the communication network media (i.e., periodicals, magazines). However, more misunderstanding and fear have been added recently to all areas of homosexual life due to the AIDS crisis. There is still a great necessity for research in this area. The paucity of research on gay fathers is the chief limitation in writing this chapter.

The role of the gay father as examined in this chapter is divided into three main sections. The first one examines the gay father as role model. The second one focuses on the child–father relationship in gay father families and discusses the disclosure of the father's homosexuality to his children. The third section focuses on the gay father family in our society. In the last section of this chapter, the child custody issue, societal discrimination, foster homes, and adoptions of children by gay men are discussed.

The Gay Father

Although the research work currently available on gay fathers is scanty, there are several studies that deal with different aspects of gay parenting. Mainly, these studies clarify the misconceptions existing in society regarding gay fathers and the relationship of them to their children. First of all, it is important to distinguish different gay fathers' lifestyles. It is commonly believed that all gay men and gay fathers manifest the same kind of behavior. However, as with heterosexual men and heterosexual fathers, research does not support this belief.

Miller (1978) studied the life structures of gay fathers and how these structures influence their fatherhood. Miller (1978) presented four lifestyles of gay fathers obtained from tape-recorded in-depth interviews conducted with forty men who rated themselves as homo-sexuals on one of the several sexual scales employed in the study. These men interacted frequently with and had legal responsibility for at least one child. The lifestyles are: "trade fathers," "homosexual fathers," "gay fathers," and "publicly gay fathers" (Miller, 1978).

Miller (1978) defined a "trade father" as the one "who engages in furtive sexual behavior with men but who is reluctant to accept this behavior as anything more than a genital urge" (p. 242) and does not consider himself as homosexual. They feel guilty because their work and the time that they spend out of the home don't allow them to maintain their parental duties. They usually have many conflicts with their wives; however, trade fathers say that they stay married mainly because of their children.

The "homosexual father" is the one "who engages in sexual be-havior with men and whose self-identity, but not public identity, is consistent with it" (Miller, 1978, p. 244). The homosexual father tries to keep his two worlds separate and attempts to develop a "clean" professional image. Like trade fathers, the homosexual fathers feel guilty because they don't spend enough time with their children. They try to cover this by giving gifts to their family and, sometimes, their gay partners. They remain with the family because of the children and the economical situation which a divorce would bring about.

"Gay fathers" are not generally living with their wives and chil-dren (Miller, 1978). They are involved in the gay social world and have a more positive attitude toward their sexual behaviors and life-styles. Gay fathers have regular schedules to visit their children. However, they are afraid that their spouses will learn about their gayness. After this is known, they feel that they may not be able to see their children again. In several cases where an individual's wife did discover his gayness, she blackmailed him and tried to control his behaviors.

"Publicly gay fathers" engage in homosexual behavior and have self-identities in accord with those behaviors. They are proud of their sexual preference. "A number of publicly gay fathers have full-time custody of their children and are living with a lover" (Miller, 1978, p. 248). Publicly gay fathers are more sedentary and do not spend much time in gay social institutions. Publicly gay fathers appear to have more problems getting custody of their children.

This research suggests that more and more trade fathers are "com-ing out" and moving toward becoming publicly gay fathers (Miller, 1978). Although "gayness is incompatible with traditional mar-riages, gayness is compatible with fathering" (Miller, 1978, p. 249).

The gay fathers[1] reported that they had a more harmonious relationship now than in their previous marital relationship. Also, their father's role gave them more satisfaction after they divorced. They also reported that their children and parents accepted their gayness more positively than their wives did. The supposition that the children are molested by fathers' gay friends or partners is not supported by this research.

The findings of Miller's (1978) study showed that the role of the gay father[2] is not always the same. It is related to the specific lifestyle of the gay father. However, it seems that the more self-aware the father is of his gayness and the more he accepts it, the better he can perform his father role.

Gay Father as Role Model

Of the gay father as role model, two beliefs are commonly held: (1) gay fathers are not positive role models for their children and (2) gay fathers will increase the amount of gayness in their children. Riddle (1978) reviewed the literature regarding the effect of gays as role models of children and regarding the development of gender identity of children during early childhood. Some of the findings were:

(1) Gender identity is extremely resistant to change after being established, even in those rare instances where biological sex is incongruent with the sex of the person.
(2) Although boys attend to same-sex models, girls are more flexible, maybe because girls are not reinforced constantly to imitate only same-sex adults.
(3) Contrary to the myth that gay men act like the opposite sex, they are more likely to model nurturant and supportive persons. They are warm and powerful adult figures with the potential for modelling a less traditional sex role for boys.
(4) Gay men are more androgynous, giving more choices to children and exposing them to greater cultural and individual concepts of diversity. From gay fathers, children learn that diverse roles are possible and can be rewarding to resist traditional sex-role socialization.

Child–Father Relationship in Gay Families

One of the fears of gay fathers is the possibility of being rejected by society, and especially by their children, wives, and relatives, if they

[1]"Gay fathers" refers to Miller's classification.
[2]Gay fathers refers to fathers, in general, whose sexual preference is toward a person of the same sex.

disclose their homosexuality. This fear increases the amount of stress and the unhappiness for gay fathers. They attempt to hide emotions and to pretend: both becoming "covers" for their sexual preference. This situation may create depression in gay fathers. Most assuredly, it limits their interpersonal relationships and does not allow them to interact with their children in a positive way.

Miller (1979) studied the nature and quality of fathering abilities of homosexual men. Miller (1979) performed interviews with men in Canadian and American cities, using a snowball sample of forty homosexual fathers and fourteen of their children. Gay fathers' ages ranged from twenty-four to sixty-four, and their children's from infants to individuals in their late thirties. None of the gay fathers in the sample became fathers in a conscious attempt to cover their homosexuality (Miller, 1979). A lot of gay fathering styles were in the sample (i.e., fathers living with their wife and children, fathers living only with the children, fathers with split custody and visiting rights).

The results in the study show that "there does not appear to be a disproportionate amount of homosexuality among the children of gay fathers" (Miller, 1979, p. 547). The sample of forty fathers had a total of forty-eight daughters and forty-two sons from which one of the sons and three of the daughters were gay. (Sexual orientations were assessed for twenty-seven daughters and twenty-one sons.) "Second generation homosexuals are rare" (Miller, 1979, p. 547). However, this particular sample of gay fathers from heterosexual parent families indicates that heterosexual parenting itself is not enough to guarantee heterosexual children.

It seems to be that wives of gay fathers notice clues indicating their husband's homosexuality but tend to deny them for different reasons (i.e., personal and social reasons). The wives of gay fathers may worry that their children will become homosexuals, and they will try to prevent gay men from parenting or seeing their children. However, the complete separation of the children from the father, regardless of his sexual preference, appears to do more harm than good (Miller, 1979). Also, father–child relationships tended to improve after the gay father moved away from the marriage situation into "openly gay lifestyles" (Miller, 1979).

Although daughters seemed to accept the gayness of the fathers better than sons, gay fathers had found that their children, boys and girls, were more positive toward them when they told them about their sexual preference than had been previously anticipated. Children stated that their father's honesty helped them to understand, strengthening the father–child relationship. However, children who showed the greatest acceptance were those who were gradually introduced to the fact that their father was gay (Miller, 1979).

Regarding father–child relationships, Mayadas and Duehn (1976) found that children ranging in age from nine to seventeen years of age (in a sample of fifteen children):

(1) Expressed little concern regarding living in a nontraditional family
(2) Perceived the stable gay family as more supportive and growth-producing than the heterosexual family
(3) Acted as advocates of their parents' lifestyles
(4) Overreacted when first informed of their parents' sexual orientation

Gay fathers, *after* disclosure to their children, tended to have a better relationship with their children and spent more time with them (Miller, 1978; Miller, 1979). Generally, gay fathers are less authoritarian, more open, and tend to use less physical punishment with their children (Miller, 1979).

Disclosure of Father's Homosexuality

It seems that the disclosure of the gay father's homosexuality to his children strengthens the child–father relationship (Miller, 1979; Bozett, 1980). Perhaps the fact that the father is honest with the children when disclosing his homosexuality to them tends to make the father a more positive figure for them. The results of studies found that children accept the gayness of their fathers more positively than was expected. However, the results showed that it is extremely hard for the wives to understand the sexual preferences and lifestyles of their husbands.

Bozett (1980) performed a study to determine why and how gay fathers disclose their homosexuality to their children. The motivation of gay fathers to disclose their sexual preference and the effect of this disclosure in the child–father relationship was evaluated with data obtained by in-depth interviews with eighteen gay fathers. Bozett (1980, p. 175) noted the following:

> Hence, for multiple reasons homosexual men may attempt a heterosexual marriage, assuming the role of husband and father. But, because of the power of a sexual drive, many of these men do eventually identify themselves as gay and assume a homosexual life style while also having the identity of father.

It was found in the study (Bozett, 1980) that the parent–child relationship is possibly the most enduring one the gay father ever experiences. It is very uncomfortable psychologically for the gay father not to disclose his sexual preference to his children. Non-disclosure creates a distance between the gay father and his children. On the other hand, disclosure seems to improve the development of a closer relationship and a better communication between the gay father and his children. However, in order to carry out this disclosure in the best, most constructive, and positive way, the father should be tolerant of others and serve as a role model of tolerance for his children (Bozett, 1980). Disclosure of the father's homosexuality to the gay father's children seems to develop a rewarding relationship. However, the right time and way to disclose his sexual preference must be considered and may vary with each specific family situation (Riddle, 1978).

Gay Father Families in Our Society

Discrimination toward gay parents is found in all social levels. Even in high socioeconomic classes many misconceptions and fears regarding homosexuality exist. It is not rare to find that the custody of a child has been granted to the heterosexual parent even though the homosexual parent was shown to be a fitter parent than the heterosexual one. There are also institutions that discriminate against gay parents and also their children because of the lifestyles of the parents. Although it seems that this situation is starting to change for the better, it will be motivated by societal necessities and forces and not necessarily by a real interest in benefits for gay people.

Child Custody Issues

Riddle (1977) reviewed different aspects of the child custody issues often confronted by gay parents. Riddle stated that very frequently judges refuse to give custody to gay parents even after they are shown to be perfectly competent parents. Research results show that difficulties with the gay parent reflect typical problems for children of divorced parents and anything that has to do with the sexual preferences of the gay parent (Riddle, 1977). In cases where the child knows about the lifestyles of the parent, it does not present specific maladjustments. Informal data indicate that the sexual preference of the gay parent does not have a negative effect on the children (Riddle, 1977). Parenting is a set of skills that people learn if they have enough motivation for it. "Sexual orientation has little to do with whether or not one wants to be a parent, but has a lot to do with motivation because of the high cost of being a gay parent at this time" (Riddle, 1977, p. 6).

Although there is the commonly held idea that gay people manifest promiscuous behavior throughout their lives, this seems to be just a stage in their lives that a segment of the gay population adopt while they are "coming out" (Riddle, 1977). Gays, like heterosexuals, prefer to form long-lasting, committed relationships, especially after the age of thirty.

Riddle also found that:

(1) There is no evidence that gay parents raise more gay children. Most gay people were raised in heterosexual families.
(2) There is no evidence that gay parents force their children to be gay. On the contrary, gay families support the child's own choice.
(3) Gay parents are aware of the necessity of the children to have adult role models of both sexes and try to maintain a steady contact with family members of the opposite sex. After early childhood, peers and significant adults, not only parents, serve as primary role models.
(4) There is no evidence that supports the belief that gays act more inappropriate in front of their children than do heterosexuals.
(5) Children will be exposed to ridicule due to the sexual preferences of their parents; however, it will give them the opportunity to learn tolerance and acceptance of differences. "Children can learn to deal more easily with teasing and intolerance than with the loss of an important parent" (Riddle, 1977, p. 11–12).

In sum, research findings suggest that the gay father can be just as fit a parent of children as the heterosexual father.

Societal Discrimination

Even though some progress has been made in understanding gay parents' child-rearing abilities, misconceptions still abound. These misconceptions are reflected in discrimination and prejudice even when these parents need and request services from public or private institutions.

Mayadas and Duehn (1976) studied gay families in order to determine principal issues regarding the gay families themselves and to evaluate social and clinical services that children in these families receive. They emphasized the need for welfare systems in the maintenance of both society and the individual. The sample in the study consisted of six gay couples (i.e., four female and two male couples). All of them had children living in the home. The couples met for six weekly, two-hour sessions with a social worker at a gay organization in a large metropolitan city.

Prior to the six sessions, there was an initial session where the principal areas of concern were stated. These areas were:

(1) Disclosure of sexual orientation to significant others (i.e., disclosure to ex-spouses and relatives, school systems, social welfare agencies and clinics, and to their children)
(2) Evolving parent–child relationships
(3) Role conflicts in gay families

The sessions were divided into four for the gay parent group and one for each family individually.

It was found in the study that the gay family feels rejection from the heterosexual-oriented society and institutions. The denial by relatives puts the gay couple in momentary crises, especially when they have to make decisions regarding special celebrations (i.e., Christmas, Thanksgiving Day). There is also denial of the existence of gay couples by social welfare and mental health agencies and by legal systems. Due to this situation, gay people and their children are often not able to recieve the services and legal support they deserve and need.

Foster Homes and Adoptions

In recent years, agencies that deal with the children in foster homes have begun to consider gay people as possible foster parents. It is important to clarify that those agencies had known the sexual preferences of potential fathers and mothers prior to the process. By itself, this is a significant change because gay people in these situations, several years ago, would not receive consideration because of their sexual preference.

Although this represents a more flexible change in agencies' policies, it is an advance in gay people's rights. This change seems to respond to a societal necessity of placing these children in homes. Some psychologists and child-development authorities reported that homosexual parents will be added to the pool of parents available for all children. They will also be used as a pool for placing gay teenagers who are very difficult to place (Saul, 1984). Therefore, more than accepting gay people's rights, these agencies seem to be trying, at the same time, to find a solution regarding children with "problems" that are hard to place in heterosexual homes.

However, in 1979 a gay couple legally adopted a two-year-old boy. Even though they stated their sexual preference, no objections were raised on the basis of sexual preference. This couple consisted of a pediatrician and a church pastor, which made stereotyped well-fit candidates for adoption. There were no negative factors that the adoption agency could address, and the decision regarding the adoption was supportive. However, this case and many others appear at this time to be isolated events. It is difficult to say what impacts these events have on changing societal attitudes relative to gay fathers.

Conclusion

Even though the gay father has not been the subject of much research, the studies available present a wide overview of the situation and issues regarding gay father parenting. The major areas discussed in this chapter are: (1) the gay father as role model, (2) the gay father–child relationship, and (3) the gay father families in society.

The main conclusions addressed by the research work dealt with these three areas. For the gay father as role model, there are different lifestyles that gay fathers adopted which influence directly their interactions with their children and their roles as parent models. As gay fathers accept themselves and others accept their gayness, they can better perform their father roles. It was found that the gayness of the gay fathers does not increase the probability of having more homosexual children. Gay fathers are more androgynous than heterosexual fathers. They provide more choices to children and expose them to cultural and individual concepts of diversity. Also, gay fathers are more nurturant and supportive persons.

Regarding the child–father relationship, it was found that it improves and develops after the gay father discloses his homosexuality to his children. There appears to be some depression when gay fathers try to cover up or hide their homosexuality from their children, limit their behaviors in front of them, and restrict free interaction with their children. Children express little concern regarding living in a nontraditional family and perceive the stable gay family as a much more supportive and growth-producing one than the heterosexual family from which they came.

In regard to the gay father families in society, it was found that even though some positive changes are occurring toward homosexuals, misunderstanding and discrimination persist. This, however, will continue to abate as additional research studies are conducted.

References

BELSKY, J. "Mother–Father–Infant Interaction: A Naturalistic Observational Study," *Developmental Psychology,* 15(6):691–697 (1979).

BOZETT, F. W. "Gay Fathers: How and Why They Disclose Their Homosexuality to Their Children," *Family Relations,* 29:173–179 (1980).

CHIBUCOS, T. R. and P. R. Kail. "Longitudinal Examination of Father–Infant Interaction and Infant–Father Attachment," *Merrill-Palmer Quarterly,* 27(2):81–96 (1981).

COLLINS, G. "A New Look at Life with Father," *The New York Times,* 30–31; 49–50; 65–66 (1979).

"Gay Male Couple Legally Adopts a Child," *Gay Community News,* Boston, MA, p. 3. (March 1979).

LAMB, M. E. "Interactions Between Eight-Month-Old Children and Their Fathers and Mothers," in *The Role of the Father in Child Development,* M. E. Lamb, ed., New York:Wiley (1976).

MAYADAS, N. S. and W. D. Duehn. "Children in Gay Families: An Investigation of Services," *The Homosexual Counseling Journal,* 3(2):70–84 (1976).

MILLER, B. "Unpromised Paternity: The Life-styles of Gay Fathers," in *Gay Men: The Sociology of Male Homosexuality,* M. P. Levine, ed., New York:Harper & Row, Publishers (1978).

MILLER, B. "Gay Fathers and Their Children," *The Family Coordinator,* 28(4):544–552 (1979).

RADIN, N. "Primary Caregiving and Role-Sharing Fathers" in *Non-Traditional Families: Parenting and Child Development,* M. E. Lamb, ed., New Jersey:Lawrence Erlbaum Associates, Publishers (1982).

RIDDLE, D. I. "Gay Parents and Child Custody Issues" (Report No. CG 012 219), Tucson, AZ: University of Arizona, Psychology Department (ERIC Document Reproduction Service No. ED 147 746) (1977).

RIDDLE, D. I. "Relating to Children: Gays as Role Models," *Journal of Social Issues,* 34(3):38–58 (1978).

ROBINSON, B. E. "Changing Views on Male Early Childhood Teachers," *Young Children,* 36(5):27–32 (1981).

ROBINSON, B. E. "Vanishing Breed: Men in Child Care Programs," *Young Children,* 43(6):54–58 (1988).

SAUL, A. "Gays and Their Right to Be Parents," *Philadelphia Inquirer,* pp. 61, 66 (1984).

SAWIN, D. B. and R. D. Parke. "Father's Affectionate Stimulation and Caregiving Behaviors with Newborn Infants," *The Family Coordinator,* 33:509–513 (1979).

U.S. Census. *Population Characteristics.* U.S. Department of Commerce, Bureau of Census (1988).

WYERS, N. L. "Homosexuality in the Family: Lesbian and Gay Spouses." *Social Work,* 32(2):143–149 (1987).

Contributors

NUMBERS IN PARENTHESES indicate the pages on which the authors' contributions begin.

GEORGIANNA M. CORNELIUS (17, 61) College of Education, Department of Curriculum and Instruction, New Mexico State University, Las Cruces, New Mexico 88003.

HARRIET E. DARLING (ix) Juniata College Early Childhood Education Center, Department of Education, Juniata College, Huntingdon, Pennsylvania 16852.

FRANCIS J. DI VESTA (135) College of Education, Division of Counseling and Educational Psychology, The Pennsylvania State University, University Park, Pennsylvania 16802.

SUZANNE KASPER GETZ (75) Licensed Psychologist, The Family and Marital Guidance Center, 727 Sir Walter Circle, Virginia Beach, Virginia 23452.

MARTHA J. LALLY (99) Department of Special Education, Counseling Department Services, Norfolk Public Schools, 800 East City Hall Avenue, Norfolk, Virginia 23501.

JUAN RAMON MORALES-FLORES (7, 173) Ph.D. Candidate, College of Education, Division of Curriculum and Instruction, The Pennsylvania State University, University Park, Pennsylvania 16802.

PEGGY E. NADENICHEK (39) Counseling Services, 441 North Spring Street, Bellefonte, Pennsylvania 16823.

SUSAN L. TROSTLE (99, 135) Department of Education, College of Human Science and Services, The University of Rhode Island, Kingston, Rhode Island 02881.

Index

EDITOR'S NOTE: Credit for developing this Index is given to Tamara L. Craig, *The Pennsylvania State University* and Elizabeth Stone, *New Mexico State University*.

187

Index